The Mother's Story

The Mother's Story

Julia O'Donnell

with Eddie Rowley

EBURY
PRESS

1 3 5 7 9 10 8 6 4 2

This edition published 2007 for Index books Ltd

Published in 2007 by Ebury Press, an imprint of Ebury Publishing

Ebury Publishing is a division of the Random House Group

The Random House Group Limited Reg. No. 954009

Addresses for companies within the Random House Group can be
found at www.randomhouse.co.uk

A CIP catalogue record for this book is available from the
British Library

The Random House Group Limited makes every effort to ensure
that the papers used in our books are made from trees that have
been legally sourced from well-managed and credibly certified
forests. Our paper procurement policy can be found on
www.randomhouse.co.uk

Printed and bound in Great Britain by Clays Ltd, St Ives plc

Hardback ISBN: 9780091917975
Paperback ISBN: 9780091918569

To my darling husband Francie

Acknowledgements

I feel very privileged to have been given the opportunity to publish this book. Here I'd like to thank Miranda West, Hannah MacDonald, Andrea Belloli and all at Ebury Press in London for their interest and hard work in making it possible.

A special thank you to my co-writer Eddie Rowley, who took me on the journey through my life and helped me to put it down on paper. Thank you, Eddie, as I couldn't have done it without you.

During the writing of the book I realized that it's not possible to mention every single person who has meant something to me, so please forgive me if your name doesn't appear. It doesn't mean I think any less of you than the ones who are named. You know I will never forget all my good friends on Owey Island. We were like one big family. So, wherever you are in the world, you have my best wishes if you are reading this. Many of my good friends from Owey, including Agnes Byrne, are now dead and gone, but remain fresh in my memory. I lost my dear friend Rose McDevitt at Christmas (2006) when she passed away after a long illness, and I miss her terribly. Rest in peace, Rose.

While the following people don't appear in the book, I want to mention them as over the years they have been such good friends to me: my Owey cousins, Mamie and Evelyn, who used to come over to the mainland for the dances and stay with me in Kincasslagh. I was always glad of their company; poor Evelyn has also passed on, so rest in peace, Evelyn; Nora O'Donnell and Susan Doogan, who were frequent visitors to my home. They'd always meet their boyfriends at my house. Susan was very tall and her boyfriend was short, while Nora was small and had a tall boyfriend. One day I said to Susan, 'Why don't you take the tall fellow?' Susan replied, 'No, I won't. The smaller the bee the bigger the buzz!' We always had good laughs. Eva and Frank in Orlando; Phyllis in California and her friends, George and Barbara in Orlando; Ian and Anne Anderson in Dundee, and Tommy and Nell Muir in Bangor, who visit us often – and Nell brings me lovely apple tarts. Andy Logue, who was a regular visitor to our house and always great company; my nieces, Grace McGonagle and Margaret Gaffney, from Dublin; Mary Assumpta Gallagher, who is my first godchild and a very special person; my darling niece Mary McGonagle. I am her godmother as well as being her grandmother; my cousins Bridie and Mary; Sheila and Carmel who come to visit on our time and go home on American time – it's always great to see you; John Martin and all my Dublin friends; Sister Finian, I remember all the lovely visits we had, and your late mother is always in my prayers; Pat and Monica; the Logue family; Brid Burke and Rosie Breen – Brid is a dressmaker and, when I don't expect it, she brings me a lovely tailor-made frock; my neighbours the Doogans; Shirley, who looks after Margaret's fan club. She always makes me feel so welcome when I go to visit; it's a home from home for me. Maire Rua, who is regarded by everyone as Daniel's number one fan. And to all of Daniel's and Margaret's fans, I want to say a big thank you; Father Pat, our parish priest, as well as Father Michael McCaughey, Father Sweeney and all priests. Special thanks to Nora McFadden in Kilcar, a very dear and kind friend who takes great care of me – and all of my friends in Kilcar; last, but not least, I'd like to thank and remember all my kind neighbours down through the years.

I hope that everything I have written in this book will bring back memories to a lot of people. And I hope they will be happy ones.

And if I haven't mentioned someone who should have been in the book, well, I just hope you'll forgive an old lady.

God bless,

Love,

Julia O'Donnell

PS: I want to express my heartfelt thanks to the people of Donegal who have voted my daughter Margaret (Margo) their Donegal Person of the Year 2006 for her contribution to music. Margaret, who received the award at a banquet this March (2007), is so thrilled to be honoured by the people of her home county.

Contents

A note from Daniel

LISTENING TO HER stories through my life, I always felt that my mother had a great book in her, and I have been encouraging her for many years to put pen to paper.

When she finally decided to write her story, I was delighted to see her set about the task with enthusiasm and passion. It provided many fruitful hours for my mother during the last two years as she documented an extraordinary life, from a poverty-stricken background to the glitz of show business.

I really feel there is no generation that will ever see change like my mother's. She was born in 1919 and has lived through so much. It would be a shame if that little bit of history went to the grave with her, as it has done with so many other wonderful characters.

Today it's hard to imagine just how primitive her early life was on the island of Owey, where she went barefoot as a child and grew up without electricity and all the mod cons we take for granted today. But it is a background rich in experiences and the traditions of a bygone age, as you will discover. Despite the hardship of their lifestyle, Owey people were enterprising, self-sufficient and a happy, close-knit community.

Later in her life, my mother had to face unimaginable personal heartbreak when my father died while still in his 40s. There were five children and we were all young.

My mother never got over my father's death. She misses him even to this day. But she put her own pain aside to ensure that we didn't suffer in any way. She sacrificed everything for us – her whole life was her family. Personally, my mother was everything to me – she was a mother and a father. Never ever did I feel a sense of missing anything in my life.

My mother wanted her family to go on and live as well as we could. She encouraged me to follow my dream, and she was always there in the background praising me. She's very, very supportive – even to this day.

I really appreciate everything that my mother has done for me and our family. And I am delighted that she has lived to see us do well in our lives – all of us, including the grandchildren; she's a very hands-on woman in their lives too.

It's good to see her enjoy the finer things in life

these days, and it gives me great pleasure to see her share in my success, just as she did with Margaret. The people who come to see me love to see her at my shows, and she enjoys the bit of fuss they make of her.

So, Mother, thank you for all that you've done through the years for me. I'm just thankful that you have been able to enjoy my success, and please God you'll make it to a hundred.

Daniel O'Donnell, 2006

I T WAS WITH great pleasure that I accepted the request to add a few words as a tribute to my mother in her book of memories. I could write for ever about this woman who is my mother, but I will keep it as short as possible. She and she alone knows how I feel about her.

My mam has stood the test of time, and we have come through a lot together. It hasn't always been plain sailing and we didn't always see eye to eye, but as I look back I think we have done okay.

I helped Mam (when Dad died) to look after the family, and I know she hasn't forgotten that. Life was lonely for her when she lost Dad, but she put all her energy into her family and did a great job.

My mother is a very strong woman; the trials of life have made her that way. She has a lot of history in her memories, and I'm so glad she is sharing them with everyone. Recently I was in Branson, Missouri, USA, where my brother Daniel was performing. He invited me up to sing on numerous occasions, and one day while speaking of Mam (as he always does) he told the audience that our mother runs the whole show from her chair in the corner. He was of course speaking of the great interest she takes in each one of our lives, and I know that keeps her so young at heart. Good luck with your book, Mam, and long may you reign.

Margo, 2006

chapter one

The Albert Hall

DRESSED SMARTLY IN a black suit, a crisp white shirt and a red tie, Joe Collum was standing in the doorway. 'Your carriage awaits you, Julia,' he announced with a big smile.

'Ah, would you get away out of that, Joe, and stop your trick-acting,' I chided.

Joe laughed.

This quiet-mannered, dark-haired man has been a member of our extended family for so long he's like another son to me.

'Do you need any help with anything?' he asked.

'Sure what would I need help with, and me only taking a handbag. After all, isn't it to the ball you're taking me?' I said.

He laughed again and led me to the hotel lift; we were heading for the car waiting outside.

Sitting in the passenger seat of the spacious people-carrier as Joe drove confidently along the side streets, I marvelled at how he could find his way around this big city of London with the bright lights of cars coming at us from all directions ... and he a native of my own quiet little corner of Ireland.

We arrive at our destination, the Royal Albert Hall, and it's like a busy airport with people racing around inside and out.

'It's a full house tonight, Julia,' Joe announced.

'Daniel will be delighted.'

'Oh, he will surely.'

Growing up on the tiny, little-known island of Owey off County Donegal on the Northwest coast of Ireland, this was never in my dreams.

Taking my seat among the colourful audience, I see men and women from all walks of life, their faces alight with excitement in anticipation of the evening's entertainment. They're all turned out in their Sunday best. Suddenly my mind is racing with so many memories.

All dolled up in my new blue dress and matching jacket, with shiny black shoes and a handbag that came all the way from Tenerife, I can't help but think how my life today is so far removed from my teenage and early adult years when I earned a wage doing hard labour picking potatoes in the fields of Scotland and gutting fish in ports far from home. Earlier this evening, as I was preparing for tonight's concert in a comfortable room of a really lovely London hotel, my thoughts wandered back to the times I slept in a cowshed at the end of a day's slave labour, the smell of the animals filling the air. A shiver runs down my spine as I recall the horrible 'visitors' we experienced in our sleeping quarters one night.

What a difference tonight's room was with its big, comfy bed, central heating, luxurious red carpet, modern wallpaper and lovely English landscapes, and all kinds of mod cons that left me baffled as to what their uses were. It was another world.

It's all so different today. So many blessings to be grateful for. Though tonight I'm reminded of a tragic event from which I will never recover. I recall the loneliness and fear that engulfed me. My life was dark and desolate back then. Had it not been for my strong religious faith, I don't know how I would have got through that very difficult time.

I look round at the sea of happy faces. All of the people seem to be transfixed by the star of the show as he takes centre stage. With every step and chorus, the applause grows louder.

The people around me occasionally nod and wave in my direction, and it's a lovely feeling. I don't know any of them – they are neither neighbours nor friends – yet they are a part of the new 'family' that has come into my life over the years. I've appeared on television, experienced the applause and warmth of audiences in venues at home and abroad, mingled with the stars of the entertainment business and been introduced to all kinds of dignitaries, including Prince Charles.

In my 87 years, I've lived two lives that have been so different it's hard to believe they've both been mine.

chapter two

The Lamp in
the Window

THE LIGHT IN the window from the tilley lamp was a lovely sight at night. It drew me to the place where I felt so secure and happy.

Our little island home was no mansion, and our family was packed in there like bees in a hive. But there was a lot of love in the house, and, for the most part, there was harmony. Well, as much harmony as you'd expect in a cottage full of young children. You'd rarely hear a raised voice from my mother or father. I think parents were probably a lot more tolerant of noise in those times, particularly as there was no television or radio. Occasionally a row would break out between my brothers as they were playing games and our mother would step in to sort it out, sometimes with the threat of a sally stick across the backs of their legs. And sometimes the threat would be carried out. I don't know what hurt those boys the most, the stinging pain from the beatings or their guilt at forcing Mother to take such drastic action to maintain order. I suspect it was the latter.

You'd hate to upset Mother because she was so good to us.

Like all the other island homes, the main living area of the small thatched cottage was a long kitchen that had an open hearth fire. Cooking pots were constantly hanging over the red-hot coals. There was a double bed covered in heavy woollen blankets in the corner, and by night the kitchen would become Mammy and Daddy's bedroom.

It was in this snug little dwelling, sitting on its own small plot of land and surrounded by other similar cottages, that I was born on 15 July 1919. There was no hospital on the island, just a midwife. God help the women if there were any complications during childbirth in those far-off times because the nearest hospital was on the mainland, and getting to it involved a nightmare half-hour trip in a small, open currach, followed by another journey in a donkey cart. And what woman in the throes of childbirth would be fit to make a sea crossing in a boat like that? So, you had to put your trust in God as you prepared to give birth, and everyone prayed – especially the very agitated father prancing up and down outside the cottage like a demented man about to face a firing squad — that mother and child would survive the act of nature.

By the time I came into the world, my mother had already come through four births and had suffered one tragedy. Her first child, my eldest sister, Bridget, died just a few days after being born on 21 August 1912. That was a terrible, heartbreaking ordeal for my poor mother and father at the start of their married life. It was a wretched period for them. I heard how my mother cried for months during this very bleak time. And of course my father felt totally unable to ease the pain. His own heart was broken too. Their only consolation was their faith. Being good God-loving people, they accepted their cross and, with the support of their kindly neighbours and the passing of time, moved on with their life. I'm sure, though, that losing a child is a trauma you never get over; you just learn to live with it. Bridget, of course, would always remain in their hearts. She was especially remembered on the anniversary of her birth.

Fortunately, Mammy and Daddy went on to be blessed with more children. James (born 1 May 1914), Edward (born 28 January 1916) and Margaret (born 7 October 1917) were already occupying the McGonagle house and creating lots of chatter by the time I came along. No doubt a sigh of relief was heard across the island when the word went round that Margaret McGonagle and her newborn daughter, Julia, were both healthy after the event. By all accounts I was welcomed into the world with a huge outpouring of enthusiasm.

'She's the loveliest wee thing the island has ever seen,' people who came to congratulate Mammy and Daddy are said to have remarked.

My mother, propped up on pillows, was no doubt beaming with delight.

'Och, she's a grand wee lass all right.' That was the comment of all the neighbours who popped their heads through the door to see the island's newest arrival, according to what I was told many years later. Wasn't it a pity that I couldn't appreciate all those flattering remarks at the time! But it's good to know at any stage that someone spoke so kindly of you.

Later the clan would see the safe arrival of the fifth and final McGonagle baby, a boy called Owen (born 18 March 1921).

Our cottage had two bedrooms. The one in the attic was occupied by my three brothers, while Margaret and I shared the other one.

By the grace of God I was born into a happy home with two of the most wonderful parents any child could wish for. Although it was a hard life for them, there was always food on our plates and laughter in the house. Everyone in our family felt loved by

Mammy and Daddy. We were secure in the knowledge that they would be there to guide and protect us during good times and bad. We had a father who worked hard to support us. He was very disciplined in the way he went about his work, and from an early stage in our young lives hard labour was laid out for us too. There was no escaping because it was a constant struggle to survive, and everyone, children as well as adults, had to toil together to get through the year.

My father, James McGonagle, was a fisherman and a great singer. He was born in America to parents who had emigrated from Ireland. His mother, originally from Magilligan in County Derry, and his father, from Owey Island, had met, fallen in love and married in America. They came home to dear old Donegal after Daddy was born, which was unusual for the times. When people left for America in those bygone days, it was rare for families back home to set eyes on them again for decades, if ever. Whenever anyone emigrated to America, the whole community would go down to the port to see them off, and it was a heartbreaking occasion. In most cases you knew they wouldn't be coming back, so there would be terrible crying. It was like a wake or a funeral.

My grandparents were among the lucky ones

who did return. They made their home on Owey Island, where my grandfather became the local postman, taking the letters over and back from the mainland. It was a hard job in those days, as he had to walk more than three miles to the post office after rowing over to the mainland in a currach. There were big parcels coming from America at that time. Relatives from the island who had crossed the Atlantic with the dream of making their fortunes, or at least carving out a better life, would send whatever they could back home to support loved ones on Owey. Postage was cheap, so my grandfather would be laden down with parcels of clothes and all sorts as he returned from an outing to the mainland.

My father grew up on Owey and was steeped in all its traditions. Daddy was a tall, striking man with a big moustache that made him look very distinguished, and hair peppered with silver specks that gradually joined up as the years passed. He always wore an unusual peaked cap that came from Scotland. He would get his shoes made by the shoemaker on the mainland, which might seem extravagant, but you can be sure that the price was right as money was so scarce in those days.

You could tell by the way the islanders behaved

around him that my father was a much-loved and well-respected member of the community. He was strong of character but very unassuming with it. Although he was a quiet man in many respects, whenever there was a hooley on the island and he was requested to sing, Daddy duly obliged to wild applause. There was no Daniel O'Donnell in those times, so Daddy was the next best thing.

Providing for a big family, even though five children was only half the size of some of the island's clans, must have been very daunting for Daddy. It was a huge responsibility, and it must have been frightening at times as the food ran out. It certainly didn't allow for any slacking off in the daily grind. Indeed, the same could be said about every other husband and father on the island. They were all hard-working men. They'd get up in the middle of the night to go fishing, and during the day they also had to attend to the bits and pieces of farming that contributed to the upkeep of their families.

My father fished lobsters during the summer months when the weather was calm. But even in the summertime he took no chances and always carried a little bottle of holy water in the currach. Everyone during those times believed in the power of prayer to keep them safe and healthy. Daddy used to cure herrings as bait for the lobsters. He often told the story of how one day as he was slicing up the herring bait and preparing the lobster pots he left a piece of herring with a knife stuck in it lying on the ground. Suddenly a seagull swooped down and took the herring with the knife away in its beak. My father had to return to the house to get another knife, and it wasn't the Lord's Prayer he said for the seagull!

As soon as the children were fit to work, it was all hands on deck to keep the family provided with food and heat. Back then everyone shared the responsibility, so Daddy had his little army of workers. From the moment we learned how to walk, we were given small jobs. There was no such thing as children being pampered in those far-off times. The work would get harder as you got older, but you were trained to do life's chores from such a young age that it was never a shock to the system, despite being almost unbearable at times.

Mammy originally came from the mainland, and she went on to the island when she married my father. My earliest memory of my mother is of her sitting in the corner frantically sewing for us children and her darling husband. She was the only dressmaker on the island at the time and the only person with a foot-action sewing machine, so her services were always in demand from neighbours. She did a lot of sewing for people on Owey, in particular for our cousins the McDevitt family, who were very close to us. There were six children in that family – Dominic, Edward, Charlie, Willie, Bridget and Mary. We were like one family as they were always in and out of our house, and we got on well together. They joined us in our games, and Willie and myself became very close as children. It was a friendship and a bond that we would maintain throughout our lives. Mammy made all the clothes for the McDevitts as their own mother couldn't turn her hand to that kind of work.

Our mother was a very quiet person who loved her home and her family. She wasn't the sort of woman who would go away visiting the neighbours to catch up on the latest gossip, she would always find something to be doing at home, where she was happiest. She was a great housekeeper.

There was a fair day over on the mainland in Dungloe on the fourth of every month, and she and my father would make the half-hour crossing over to it in a currach. They would spend several hours sifting through the street stalls for bargains, and rarely would they come away empty-handed. They weren't after luxuries or personal treats. They'd pick up cheap overcoats which my mother would rip apart when she got home, washing them and making our clothes with the material – suits for the boys and skirts for me and Maggie. Mammy never bought anything in that market other than an item of clothing she could make into some kind of an outfit for her children. She was a genius at sewing, really gifted with her hands. When we got flour for baking our bread, it came in large 8-stone bags. When the bags were empty, she would wash and then dye them and make lovely dresses for us. Four bags would make sheets for the beds, so she never had to buy any material. She'd knit big socks for us that we'd wear if the weather was extremely cold in the winter. And we'd go barefoot during the summer and autumn. We'd wear those socks till April, when the temperature would start to rise again.

'What do you think of that?' my mother would ask, displaying one of the garments she had designed and made from clothing she'd picked up in the market.

'That's grand. Just grand,' we'd say.

Mammy would smile, satisfied with the fruits of her work. Then she'd store away the garment until it was needed. Nothing was ever worn without a good reason. Everything was saved until it was absolutely essential to use it.

In the summertime my father went over to Kincasslagh every Saturday to sell his lobsters, and then he'd buy the week's groceries from the shop. My mother always ordered 2 pounds of mince for our Sunday dinner. After eating fish every day during the week, it was a great treat. One day my father bought the mince and then slipped into Logue's pub for a beer as a little treat for himself. He left his bag of shopping outside because in those times you never had to worry about it being stolen, certainly not in that part of the world anyway.

However, when he came out, Daddy was horrified to see the tail end of a dog sticking out of the bag of groceries. The dog's tail wagging wasn't a good sign. Sure enough, after Daddy gave the dog a kick up the backside and sent him racing off down the street, he discovered that all the mince had been eaten by the mutt. What was he going to do? He didn't have enough money to buy more mince. And he couldn't face going home to tell everyone what had happened. He obviously felt really stupid that he had left the meat lying around to tempt any animal. He could hardly blame the dog; he didn't know any better. So on his return home he told a little white lie to my mother, claiming that the shop had run out of mince. As he looked round the kitchen Daddy could see a row of little faces all looking so disappointed. He must have felt as small as a Jack Russell at that moment. We had fish again that Sunday, and it was only with the passing of time that Daddy told the true story of the scavenging dog that took advantage of a man's thirst for a pint.

As children we enjoyed a lot of freedom on Owey. Island life was carefree in the sense that parents never had to worry about their children coming to any harm from another human being. Nowadays people don't know their neighbours a few doors away from them. There was no stranger on the island in our time. Neither were there any secrets among the houses; everyone knew what the other one was up to. You could walk through the door of any house uninvited. There was no such thing as knockers on doors; you just walked in, and you were welcome. And you could trust every man, woman and child. There were no bad fellows on the island. Everyone looked out for each other and supported each other. If someone took ill during the night and needed a doctor, all the houses would light up their lamps, and the people would spill out into the darkness to help. There were four men on standby every night in case of an emergency. They were designated as the men who would row the boat to the mainland. Everyone else would help out with the preparations and lead the way to the boat by the light from their lanterns.

Owey had 30 houses, and we were related to a number of the families: the McGonagles, the Gallaghers and, as I mentioned, the McDevitts. Even though the houses were small, many of them accommodated huge numbers of offspring. There were a dozen in some cottages between parents and children. You'd wonder how such small cottages could accommodate so many. It was like a magic illusion as a never-ending stream of people would file out of one family home. It's amazing how people can adjust to their surroundings when they have to.

You'd wonder how the mothers and fathers didn't go mad with so many children in the house, but in those times, long before television and video and DVD were heard of, us children were very inventive in finding ways to amuse ourselves. We'd herd the cows home from the fields around 11 a.m. during the summer. After they were milked, the animals were tied in until 3 p.m., and then we'd go back out to the fields with them and play our games there.

In the summertime the sun would be glistening on the surface of the clear blue sea as we carefully made our way along the well-worn island path with the cows. Sometimes I'd let out a yelp after stepping on a sharp pebble. On days like that, the water sparkled like a huge diamond ring: the rays shooting on to the sea looked like they were sending messages from heaven.

Owey Island during the summer is the most beautiful and magical place in the world. It was so eerily quiet, you could nearly hear the grass growing between the stones. Skipping along the pathways as a child, I took the scenic beauty and the unusual inlets that nature had carved out for granted.

There is one particular rock formation that as children we were led to believe was a giant's chair. You had to crawl carefully across rocks to reach it. I only did that the one time because getting off it is a very dangerous manoeuvre, and I got a fright when I nearly slipped. I was terrified because I could so easily have fallen to my death on the rocks below. The giant's grave is said to be at a nearby spot. Stones marked the head and the feet, and no grass ever grows in between, so folklore has it.

Before heading off with the cows, we'd steal an egg or two from underneath our hens and take them with us to the mountain. Just one egg provided many hours of fun. We'd place it a few yards in front of us, and then one of us would be blindfolded. Using a stick, that player had to attempt to hit the egg. Each of us took a turn, and whoever broke the egg with the stick was deemed to be the winner. An egg might last for five days before somebody would strike it.

Another popular form of amusement involved wee rabbits which could be found hopping around in the vicinity of the mountain. Because they were small, the young rabbits were easy to catch by hand. You'd make a run at them and grab them in a diving tackle. Then we used them to play a game. A square was formed with sticks on the ground, and then we'd wet the wee rabbits in a nearby lake. When they were wet, they weren't able to run for some odd reason. A rabbit was then placed in the centre of the square, with a player at each corner. As the rabbit began to dry off, he'd start to get a new lease of life, and whichever side he raced to, the player on that side had to try to catch him. The person who was first to catch the rabbit was declared the winner. Now people might think that was cruel to the wee rabbits, but there was no harm in it at all. We'd always let them hop away afterwards, and I doubt they suffered any trauma as we took great care to handle them gently.

We played marbles a lot too. Three holes would be poked in the ground, and then you'd try to flick the marbles into them. Those were all simple pastimes, but we enjoyed them as we knew nothing better.

Santa Claus, of course, would visit the island every Christmas, but he didn't have a big sack back then. The presents were very modest, especially by today's standards. I remember one Christmas Santa left me an apple and a bar of chocolate. Another time Maggie and myself got wee sets of cups and saucers. An aunt in America sent us dolls once. They were the prettiest things with lovely hair, nice shoes and gorgeous clothes. But we weren't allowed to spoil them. After a day or two they were hung up in the kitchen for show. Everyone who came into the house admired those two dolls. Maggie and myself would sit and gaze at them too but with a feeling of fierce frustration. All we wanted to do was hug those dolls, comb their hair, and undress and dress them up again. We just wanted to play with them. But like our good clothes and good shoes, we were never allowed to spoil them.

It wasn't all fun and games, of course. As I mentioned, we all had our jobs to do as well. Everyone on the island had a small farm. It was nothing to brag about, just enough to provide a family with vegetables, including potatoes, turnips, carrots, cabbage and other produce. We were very self-sufficient on the island for the most part. It was only small luxuries that were occasionally brought over from the mainland.

Although there are many great memories, especially as the passing of time seems to play tricks with the mind and you only seem to recall the good things that happened, I don't have a romantic notion about all of my life on the island. It was very hard most of the time, even when we were young children. I still remember the excruciatingly painful blisters on my hands from kibbin' potatoes. The ground was like concrete, and you'd be down on your hands and knees with a kibbin' iron, which was like a trowel, scooping out the soil to sow the potato seeds. I was only about ten or eleven years old at the time, but when I'd look at my hands they were like old people's because they were covered in blisters and welts. Sometimes I'd feel so miserable working outdoors in the cold and the wet, or in the scorching sun, that I'd be praying for the day to end. But you'd never complain to anyone. This was normal life. I'd look around at all the other kids, and they were doing the same chores as myself. You'd be sowing corn, making hay, setting turnips or pulling carrots. There was always something to be done around the farm, even though it was small. There was no joy in it at all, but because all of the other kids of my age were working hard too, it never made me feel that I was some kind of a victim.

As soon as I was old enough to help my mother around the house, I willingly attended to my chores. I never tired of housework. I actually enjoyed it, so it was no bother to me. I loved helping Mammy, and she never had to ask for anything to be done. I knew the things that had to be taken care of and went about doing them without giving it a second thought. It's not that I was striving to be a good girl and trying to earn praise from Mammy. It's just the way things were; you knew that you were expected to do whatever had to be done. There was no sitting in front of a television or playing with all kinds of gadgets that children have today. It was mainly chores that filled the time for us young folk on the island.

One of my earliest household jobs was washing the clothes. Monday was wash day in every house on the island. All during the week a pile of clothes would grow and grow and form a mini-mountain in a corner; it would have sheets that were stripped off the beds as well as the dirty clothes that had been worn by members of the family.

There was no electricity in those days and no mod

cons like a washing machine or spin dryer. The washing was done by hand in a bath, using a washboard and plenty of elbow power. The water was heated in a pot over the fire, and you'd use Sunlight soap or carbolic soap and a fistful of washing soda to get out the stains. I'd scrub like crazy, working my hands to the bone on the really nasty stains that were picked up from the daily grind on the island and from the fishing. I'd carry the wet clothes to a nearby ditch, where I'd carefully spread them out to dry. When you looked around the stone ditches on a Monday afternoon, it was like carnival time. All the different sheets and coloured clothes in all shapes and sizes were spread out near every family's home. They could be seen for miles around and were like flags in the distance.

Naturally, living on an island, we survived mainly on fish supplemented by home-grown vegetables. It was a healthy diet, with all natural produce and no insecticides or chemical sprays used during the growing. There was no such evil as cancer in those times, so we were better off in that respect. We were rarely ill.

My father used to go over to the mainland in March and April and pull a weed called bogbine out of a lake. It was big, with long stalks, and he'd bring it back over to the island. My mother would boil it, put treacle on it and bottle it. We were forced to drink a glass of that every morning before we went to school. It was disgusting to taste, but you had to take it. They said it purified the blood and that's why people weren't getting sick.

No one went hungry on the island, despite the poverty, although food was always dished out sparingly. It was shared among the little community, so there was comfort in knowing that your family, neighbours and friends would rally round when the going got tough. If a neighbour's cow was in calf and had gone dry, you'd share your milk with that family. We all looked out for each other. We always had that security. Everyone made sure to take care of the old people who lived alone in their houses. When the weather was good, family members would go out once or twice a week to shop on the mainland. Whoever was going out for the groceries would always call to the old people to see if they needed anything. Sure all they'd be asking for was a dozen of soft biscuits, which you'd get for a penny. When I'd go out, I'd take back seven or eight dozen biscuits for all the old folk, and that would make them so happy. We'd also do chores for them, like bringing in their turf and lighting their home fires for baking and warmth. You'd take them milk after the cows were milked.

I had an aunt living on the island, a small but hardy little woman dressed all in black, who was 90 years old and still living on her own. I took milk to her every night after we milked our cow. She'd always be sitting alone by the turf fire when I called with the milk. There'd be a pan hanging on the crook over the fire and a cake of bread baking in it. A little enamel mug would be sitting among the hot coals and tea brewing in it. Then she'd have her tea and the hot bread straight from the pan while I sat and chatted with her for company. No old person ever had to worry about being left to fend for themselves. They were all loved and treated with respect.

My paternal granny was one of the old people. She lived till she was very, very old. Her little cottage was a good distance from our home, and when she reached old age she wasn't able to walk down to see us. Granny loved to visit us, so we'd be sent to fetch her in a wheelbarrow. We'd gather round and lift her into it. Then she'd lie back with her legs sticking out over the end and hold on to the sides for dear life as we wheeled her down the path in full view of everyone. It wasn't a very dignified mode of transport for a lady, but she didn't seem to mind. That's just the way it was in those times. You had to be inventive and use whatever tool was available to get the job done.

Granny would stay for the day, eat with us and enjoy every mouthful of fish on her plate. The fish was boiled, or if it was herring it would be roasted on a grill suspended over the open fire in the kitchen. It was accompanied by a big, black pot of potatoes, which were also boiled over the fire and set aside until the herring was ready to be eaten. When her belly was full and her time was up, Granny would be put back in the wheelbarrow and taken home again. She'd have a smile on her face as the barrow rolled along the stony path. We'd take turns to wheel it, and there was always someone walking each side in case it toppled over. You wouldn't want your granny falling out of a wheelbarrow.

My mother always prepared lovely meals for us. In her young days, before she got married, she was a cook in the Industrial School in Killybegs, County Donegal. She gained great experience there, and it served us well as a family. We looked forward to the meals she created, and we'd devour them in seconds when we came home ravenous from school.

In the wintertime we'd have a fish called baiyan on weekdays. When my father came home from a fishing outing with his catch, he'd salt the baiyan, and then they'd be washed and hung on lines to dry out. They'd be kept for winter use when fishing became more difficult, if not impossible, due to the atrocious weather.

I remember how one time there was a storm that lasted for 19 days. It blew the roof off some of the houses, as well as the post office, and none of the boatmen were able to leave the island to bring in supplies because the sea was raging. As you always expected some kind of a storm at that time of the year, you'd have stocked up with extra supplies. We had plenty of potatoes and fish, milk and butter, and we had an 8-stone bag of Milford flour so we could bake our own bread. I remember, though, that the men ran out of cigarettes and got very cranky without their smokes.

Some people were so poor that they weren't able to buy enough food to put in store for the long winter months. Anyone who had a bit of money to spare would buy extra supplies and give some to those people. There were a lot of islanders who depended on the generosity and kindness of their neighbours. I recall one woman coming to our door looking for flour amid that terrible storm. My mother had just one bowl left by this time but even though she had no idea how much longer the storm was going to torment us, she gave away half the flour to the neighbour. The following day the storm suddenly died down and allowed the men to make a trip to the mainland for fresh supplies. It appeared as if her good deed had been repaid by the Lord above.

When I was a young girl I was always very good at scavenging an extra bit of food. There was an old couple and their bachelor son who lived nearby to our cottage. I knew the time they had set for their dinner, so occasionally I'd drop in for a visit coming up to it. I'd sit in the corner, watching the fish sizzling over the fire. The people in the house seemed to enjoy having my company, but I was only there for the grub. I'm not certain if they ever noticed that the time of day I called happened to coincide with their main meal.

'Would you eat a bit of fish?' the old lady would always ask.

'Is there a bit to spare?' I'd have the cheek to ask in return.

'Ah, sure, your name is on one of them,' the woman of the house would laugh. Maybe they knew my game after all.

We always had a nice big fire in our home, and sometimes we'd sit around it at night eating crab toes that my mother would roast for us over the coals. Mother always made a pot of cocoa at night, and she'd leave it sitting in the hot ashes. Then, just before going to bed, we drank that delicious cocoa. Before we went to bed in the winter, my mother would heat the lid of a pot in the hot coals. Then she'd wrap a blanket around it and use it to warm up our beds. There were very few luxuries during those harsh times, but a cup of cocoa and a hot bed on a cold winter's night was heaven on earth to us. She was a thoughtful mother, and even though the times were hard she tried to give us little comforts. It's those acts of kindness that made us realize just how loved we were in that island home.

As I got older, my day during the summer would start at 3.45 a.m., when I got up to cook breakfast for my father and some of the other fishermen before they set off to haul in the lobster pots from the sea. It was a simple breakfast of just two boiled eggs for each man. There were no big fry-ups in those days.

'Thanks, Julia, you're a great wee girl,' my father would say as he left the cottage and headed off out into the darkness.

The men went off to fish at that very early hour of the morning so that they could make two hauls on the same day, the second one taking place in the evening. When they left in the morning, I didn't hop back into bed to catch a couple more hours of sleep, even though I was quite entitled to do just that. I loved working in the home, so I would find something to occupy myself before the sun came up. Sometimes I'd churn buttermilk, and I'd have the butter ready before my mother got out of bed.

'God, Julia, you're a great wee worker,' my mother would say.

Those few words of praise from Mammy were worth more to me than all the money in the world.

Later in the morning I'd strap up the donkey and go away to the mountain to draw a load of turf for the fire. The turf had already been cut, dug out of the ground, dried and stacked. I'd take a couple of loads back to the house to keep the fire burning for cooking.

The well for drinking water was a long distance from our home, so I'd have to make several trips a day to fetch it in buckets. I'd fill a wooden barrel that sat outside our door. The barrel was never allowed to run dry in the summertime because the heat of the sun would split the wood. So I had to make sure that it was constantly topped up.

There were two wells, one for drinking water and another that was used for washing tatties and clothes. It was no easy task to retrieve the water from the wells. I had to get down on my knees with a wee saucepan and scoop it up to fill the bucket. It was a chore that seemed to take for ever. Everyone on the island used the same two wells, so you'd always have neighbours waiting their turn. Despite this, there was never any friction. No one was in a hurry. There was no one watching a clock on Owey.

There was no church on our island, so we had to go to the mainland in a currach to attend Sunday Mass as well as for funerals, weddings and baptisms. We did, however, have a little schoolhouse, which was built in 1911, and two teachers. I was just four years old when I started my education there, but it wasn't traumatic. The school was close to my home, and I was surrounded by children I knew, because living on an island we were like one big family. There was no such thing as a school uniform. But I did have a good cardigan and skirt and neat, short hair. I probably didn't look any different from all the other little people in the room that day. No doubt I was aware that I was going into a strange new world. I'd never been in the same room with so many children before. And we all had to listen to and obey the adult standing at the top of the room. He was called Teacher. I have no real memory of those early years in that little schoolhouse, so it can't have been too bad.

As I got older and was expected to absorb all the information that the teachers tried their best to get us to learn, I'm sure I let them down many times. I have no doubt that they were frustrated with me. I was bright and should have been a better pupil. It's just that I didn't have any enthusiasm for what school had to offer. I have to confess that I didn't have the same dedication that I applied to my work in the house and on the farm. This, of course, occasionally got me into trouble.

There were forty of us in the school, and the two teachers ruled with a stick and a strap. I never had a great interest in lessons like history, geography and maths. And I have to admit that I spent my time copying answers to mathematical questions from some of the others. I was never going to be a star student, that was obvious to the teachers. And I did get some beatings. Today I hold no grudges against those teachers. Whatever punishment I received was through my own fault. And corporal punishment was quite acceptable in those times. There was no such thing as running home and complaining to your parents. You wouldn't tell them that you had got a hammering because then you'd be admitting that you had done wrong. If you learned your lessons and did what you were told, you wouldn't get a beating. So I have no one to blame but myself for any hammerings I received from the teachers.

I didn't get regular beatings, but there was one day I got 84 slaps between my two hands; that's something I've never forgotten. I was studying to receive the sacrament of confirmation at the time, but I hadn't bothered to learn my catechism. My turn came to be asked a question, and I hadn't a notion what the answer was.

'Julia McGonagle,' the teacher said with a raised voice.

I lifted my head after several seconds of silence.

'Come up here this minute.'

I left my desk and shuffled to the top of the classroom.

'If you had bothered your head to study your catechism last night you'd know the answer. Now I'm going to give you something to remember.' The teacher had clearly lost his temper with frustration; his face was red with rage as he reached for the long leather strap.

I held out my right hand and took my punishment. It seemed to go on for an eternity.

The teacher stopped and glared at me. There wasn't a tear to be seen in my eyes. I had accepted what had been dished out to me with courage. I was feeling proud of myself when he nodded and said, 'Now the other hand.'

Well, I nearly died on the spot at the thought of having to endure the same pain again on my left hand. But I had no choice and slowly put out my hand and took my beating. This time round, the teacher was certain that I had learned my lesson. Tears welled up in my eyes.

It was cruel, certainly, by today's standards.

One of the teachers was from the mainland, and he'd come over to the island to give us classes. We'd be cheering with delight on days when the sea was too rough for him to make the crossing. In the winter months there were days when no boat could travel back and forth. That was always good for us children. We didn't realize at the time that they were probably the best days of our lives. Try telling that to any child. It's only in adulthood that you realize those things.

God forgive us, but we used to be delighted if somebody not related to us died during the school term because that meant no school. You'd be laughing if you heard that a distant relative had died because you'd have three days off.

No one was ever buried on the island. Their remains were taken over by boat to the mainland, and then six men would carry the coffin from the port on the two- or three-mile journey to the chapel, then on to Cruit cemetery after the funeral Mass. Before that, the deceased were waked on the island for two days, and, believe it or not, there was always great fun at a wake, particularly at night. People would be telling stories, and there would be a lot of trick-acting going on among the younger people. I remember how there used to be a quiz and if a girl missed a question she had to kiss some old man at the wake. That was funny, 'cos none of the girls wanted to be kissing an old man.

The corpse would be washed and laid out on a bed. White curtains would be hung around the bed and three black crosses placed on the covers, one to the left, one to the right and one in the centre. Then a boat would be sent to the mainland to fetch a simple wooden coffin. The body wouldn't be put in the coffin until the day of the funeral.

Anyone who could leave the island would attend the funeral. You'd be sad seeing someone from Owey going away in a coffin.

There was one couple on the island who were always fighting. They didn't have a happy marriage but had stayed togther despite their differences. Eventually, the wife died. It was the general custom that when a coffin was leaving a house it was carried out feet first.

'Wait there a minute!' exclaimed the widower as

a group of neighbours struggled to manoeuvre the box out of the little cottage.

The coffin bearers halted on the spot.

'Turn her round so that she can see the inside of the house as thank God she won't be coming back,' the widower added with a smug smile.

As there was no electricity or central heating in the schoolhouse, we all went to school with a sod of turf under each arm in the winter for the solid-fuel fire in the classrooms. We went home for our lunch in the summer, but during the winter we were kept in, and the teachers gave us cocoa with loaf bread and home-made butter. There was a lovely taste from the butter; you wouldn't get the like of it today.

In those days when locals had calves they'd kill them, cure them and then share the meat among all the houses on the island. The calves weren't worth any money on the mainland at the time. A local called Andy Shamie killed a calf one day and, like his neighbours, shared it with kin community. It meant that every home had meat to eat during the week instead of fish. We all went home for our school break and had our dinner, as we called the midday meal.

When we went back to school, the teacher came into the room, took a match out of a matchbox and started picking his teeth.

There was one cheeky little fella in the class who always had a comment to pass, even when he wasn't asked for one. 'Sir, I know what you're picking out of your teeth,' he shouted up at the teacher.

'What am I picking out of my teeth?' the teacher asked.

'A bit of Andy Shamie's calf,' the little fella replied.

The class laughed.

The teacher turned to the boy who'd made the smart comment. 'Come up here now,' he said, reaching for the leather strap, 'and I'll give you something you won't find so funny.'

I'm sure the boy in question has never forgotten Andy Shamie's calf.

During schooldays you'd get home around 3 p.m., and then you'd go out to do your work on the farm. Or we'd have to go down to the sea, when the tide was out and the rocks were exposed, to pull dulse, a seaweed that was edible and full of goodness. We'd head off in a currach with my father and gather as much dulse as we could by climbing over the rocks along the coast, maybe three or four bags at a time. It was very hard work, but it contributed to the family income as my father would sell a sack of dulse on the mainland for half a crown.

The spring work on our little farms started on 18 March, the day after St Patrick's Day. And you did whatever was laid out for you without question. Some days we'd be sent off to the sea to gather winkles among the rocks. At that time of the year it was always very chilly, and that was a hard job, sifting through the rocks in the freezing-cold weather. My mother used to give us old socks, with the toes cut off, and we'd wear those gathering winkles. They were to keep our feet warm, but our toes were exposed so that we'd be able to get a grip on the rocks and not fall as we went about our work. We moved fast to keep warm as we gathered the winkles in a bucket. We had to fill a large sack and that was then sold, fetching 1s 6d. If we gathered two bags of winkles it was considered to be a good day's work.

We used to run and work barefoot on the island during the summer, but my father would buy shoes for us at Hallowe'en. 'Them has to do yez now till April,' he'd say.

But as I got older I'd be secretly away dancing on the island at night when I was supposed to be sleeping, and I'd wear the soles off those shoes.

My father never got angry. Instead, he'd salvage old tyres off bicycles and use the rubber to make new soles for our footwear. 'Now,' he'd say, passing over his handiwork, 'good as new, though I don't know how you wear them out so quickly.'

Oh, the guilt I felt then about my secret excursions into the night.

chapter three

Mass, a Hooley and Poteen

S UNDAY ON THE island was a mixed blessing. Apart from the milking of the cows, the Sabbath was strictly a day of rest on Owey. You were forbidden from doing any fishing, knitting or other jobs that weren't essential. It was also the only day that children would get to wear their 'good' shoes. We were only allowed to wear them for Mass in the village church on the mainland.

Without fail, unless there was sickness or stormy weather, Sunday involved a trip in the currach to Mass in the little chapel at Cruit.

I have a very strong faith today, and my religion has been a great comfort to me throughout my adult life, but in my young days on the island it didn't have the same appeal. In fact, there were times when I found it to be a very hard discipline. In order to receive the sacrament of Holy Communion at Mass at that time, you had to be fasting from midnight the night before. Mass was at 11 a.m. on a Sunday, and I dreaded that trip in the wintertime. You'd leave the island just after 9 a.m., starving because breakfast wasn't allowed, and everyone, adults and children, would be dressed up in their Sunday best. Myself and my sister Maggie had only one pair of Sunday shoes between us. On the day that I'd wear them she'd stay home to mind the cows.

All of us children would go down to the currach in our bare feet as we weren't allowed to put on our good shoes until we reached land on the other side. In hail, rain or snow we went barefoot to the currach. The adults would get into the boat, and then we had to push it out into the sea for them. Afterwards, I'd sit there trembling with the cold and my feet would be like two lumps of ice. I'd glance down at them as the boat bobbed up and down on the waves during the half-hour ride, and they'd have turned blue from the cold. When we reached land it was our job to jump out into the sea again and pull in the currach. All the adults would then get out and we'd walk the 3 miles to the chapel, the children still suffering in silence as we plodded along in our bare feet. We wouldn't be allowed to put on our shoes until we were just below the chapel. None of our parents saw any harm in us going without shoes for that weekly outing to Mass. We were young, strong and healthy, and shoes were not easy to come by as money was so tight. It was most important to take care of our shoes for Sunday Mass, so a little bit of hardship just had to be endured for that purpose.

Mass usually lasted for about an hour, during which time you'd start to feel a tingling sensation in your feet again as they warmed up. But then, just as you were enjoying the pleasure of that, you had to remove your shoes and start the torture all over again on the trip home.

At least on the return journey you'd be looking forward to what was awaiting you back at home. As soon as you got out of the currach you'd smell the cooking. Whoever stayed behind would have the meal well under way by the time you returned. And I can tell you it was very welcome when you hadn't eaten since before midnight on the previous day. The food would consist of wee chickens we'd have reared, or of mince, and carrots, onions, turnips, cabbage and potatoes. The potatoes would be smothered with home-made butter, and the whole lot washed down with fresh milk. That was a feast you'd really enjoy after the morning's excursion.

On Sundays when you couldn't make the sea crossing, two rosaries were said in every house on Owey, the first one at 11 a.m. to coincide with the Mass. My mother headed the rosary in our home, and on a Sunday she would end it by saying, 'I offer up the rosary this day with the priest's intention that we may gain the benefit of the Mass.' On Sundays and on every other day of the week, there was a rosary said at 10.30 or 11 p.m. before we went to bed.

My father was very religious and would go down on his knees to say his nightly prayers before getting into bed. As soon as he awoke the following morning, the first thing Daddy would do was get down on his knees again and say his morning prayers. I firmly believe there was a lot more devotion to God in those days.

It was the custom for children to visit every home on Owey Island on Easter Sunday – and you'd get an egg in each house, unless, of course, the family had no hens. You could keep all the eggs for yourself and eat them until they ran out. That was a real treat because normally the island children wouldn't get an egg to eat for breakfast as they were sold to the shop on the mainland to pay for the groceries. I remember how some families would have up to three dozen hens and, of course, a rooster. The rooster was the king of the flock. He was like a father to his children, and the hens had to obey his orders. Sometimes an egg would have two yolks, so that would be a double treat. All of us children felt it was a terrible shame that Easter came only once a year.

It wasn't all religion and prayer on the island, though. There was a lot of fun to be had too. As I got older, I lived for the third Sunday of the month. Every three weeks, on that day, a hooley was held in our local school. It was a day to forget all about our troubles, our worries and our hard times. It was a day to let our hair down and be free to enjoy the music and the dancing. Lots of people, including the local priest, would travel over from the mainland for the day of festivities, and nobody ever went away hungry.

Everyone on the island would work together preparing food for all the party-goers. All the women would bake bread with flour, and sometimes raisins would be included among the ingredients. The bread cakes were baked in an oven set amid the hot coals on the open hearth fire. You'd put a lid on the oven and coals over the lid. And that bread was the most delicious you ever tasted when it was served up with tea.

The schoolhouse, which had been cleared of desks, would come alive to the sound of the tin whistle, melodeon and fiddle that day; it was the greatest music you ever heard. All the adults and children flocked there to enjoy it, and it was a real celebration of life. The Irish dancing was just so exciting to watch and do; there was hardly a person on the island who couldn't do the steps. Long before anyone had heard of Michael Flatley or *Riverdance*, it was a huge part of our lives. We all learned to keep in step, and you'd be laughing with the joy of it as you kicked up your heels. It was definitely the highlight of every month.

Every 23 June was the annual summer party on the island. We always had a big bonfire on that night and everyone, young and old, would gather round it for a singsong. St Patrick's Day was another great day of celebration, of course, and we'd all leave the island for various events on the mainland. The day would start off with Mass in Kincasslagh, and then we'd enjoy the local band competition before going on to nearby Annagry for a dance at night. We all got 2s 6d each to spend that day. Sometimes we had a few pence left over to take back home. None of the young folk drank alcohol. It was 3d into Gandey's dance hall. We got our tea in Mary O'Brien's in Dungloe for 6d, which was our food of the day. There was always a lot of fun, so we looked forward to that day all year.

The night before St Patrick's, everyone would prepare their best clothes. All the boys would have their white shirts starched and ironed, and lovely ties laid out to complement them; their shoes were so well polished you could use them as a mirror, and their hair would be slicked back and styled with some kind of gel.

One St Patrick's Day my cousin Jim McGonagle was in tears because his granny had died. He wasn't heartbroken because she had gone … it was the fact that his big day had been spoiled as he couldn't go to the dance! I was left to take care of the house while his mother and father went to the wake. Our granny – his other granny – was living in the house and Jim turned to her and said, 'Isn't this terrible? Had she no other day to die, only today? Look at all my clothes ready there for the dance, and now I can't go. This is shocking. Couldn't she have waited?'

Granny never said a word. She could see that Jim was taking his disappointment very badly indeed.

Then he looked up at Granny again and whinged, 'I suppose you'll die next Easter and spoil that day for me too.' And he was being serious.

Granny never said a word, but I suspect she was laughing her heart out inside.

There was no crime on Owey, but every now and then the Garda would come over from the mainland looking for poteen, which was the island's whiskey and which was illegal to distil. Barley was grown for the making of poteen, and potatoes would be used on occasion. The men enjoyed their sup of poteen particularly when there was a dance on the island. They'd all be drunk on nights like that.

Poteen was also another source of local income as it was sold on the mainland even though it was against the law. But no one on the island ever saw any real harm in it. They always said that it should never have been outlawed. Well, I suppose when it comes to drink, some people never see any harm in it, especially the men. That's not to say, however, that they weren't aided and abetted in their illegal brewing and storing by their womenfolk, my own mother included.

There was always a danger that the Garda would slip on to the island and pounce on the illegal distillers, so the poteen-makers became very inventive in the way they hid or camouflaged their precious liquid. A big copper device, known as a worm, was used to make the poteen. One time when the Garda came sniffing around on the island, my mother hid the worm for the poteen-makers under a heap of manure, and the police never found it.

There was a local man, a big fella with a long, shaggy beard, who had his poteen in a huge barrel outside his cottage. When he heard the Garda unexpectedly coming over the bay one day, he flew into a panic. How was he going to hide his illegal brew? As the distressed poteen-maker thought about the imminent threat to his cherished supply of alcohol, he realized he had few, if any, options. The one that stared him in the face was one he didn't want to contemplate. It seemed that the only way to stop the Garda catching him with the poteen was to turn the barrel over and pour it out. That would break his heart after all the hours and hard work he had put in distilling the drink. As the very stern-looking Garda approached his cottage, the huge man hopped up on the barrel to keep his secret store away from their senses. His ploy worked, and the lawmen passed on without spotting the poteen right under their noses. They obviously thought the man was sitting on a barrel of water. He was feeling very smug until he tried to get off the barrel. To his embarrassment he discovered that his big, fat backside was stuck in it. He couldn't draw attention to himself by shouting for help, so he had to sit there for hours until the Garda were gone and he was able to alert the neighbours to his plight. Then it took a couple of amused local men to prise him off his poteen. He never did live that incident down.

Some people used the poteen as a form of medicine. They'd even give it to their children as punch.

Hot poteen, which was made with milk, butter and sugar, was given to children to sip as a cure for colds and flu. Taken in this form it was even said to be good for rheumatism. Some women on the island swore it kept them in good health right through their old age.

It wasn't just for poteen that the Garda would occasionally come calling to the island. If you kept dogs, they'd be checking that you had a licence for them. Whenever we saw the Garda coming, someone would take the dogs away to the hills and keep them out of sight until the Garda were satisfied that they'd seen all there was to be seen.

One day, however, a neighbour was caught without a dog licence. We were all out digging tatties when we saw the Garda coming to serve the summons, so we quickly gathered a heap of stones and went down to the shore where their boat was set to come in. As soon as the Garda got near to the shore, a whole crowd of us started throwing stones at them until eventually they gave up, turned the boat round and went away. That summons was never served.

At night on the island we'd go visiting other houses, and as children we'd sit and listen enthralled as our elders regaled us with wonderful stories of times past. The old people also terrified us with great ghost stories that had been handed down from generation to generation. They were so scary and realistic that you'd be rattling with fear on the way back home. We used to take a burning sod of turf out of the fire in the house we'd been visiting and stick a wire in it; that was our lantern to show us the way home.

The roads were good on Owey because we eventually got grants from the council to keep them maintained. They were stone roads, and they snaked their way round the island. Owey was well looked after by everyone, and a fine, manicured garden on a grand estate wouldn't have matched its neat appearance.

There were also grants available for the roofing of houses. My father availed himself of one to slate our thatched cottage. To qualify for a grant, you had to be able to speak Gaeilge, the Irish language. My father first got a grant to slate the roof over the bedroom. Some time later, he applied for another grant to slate the roof over the kitchen.

The grant man came over to the island and asked my father, 'Have you any Gaeilge?'

'Well,' replied my father, 'I had enough to put a roof on the room, so surely to God I have as much again as would put a roof on the kitchen.'

The tall and very important-looking grant man

sucked on his cigarette, removed it from his lips and burst out laughing, creating a cloud of smoke.

My father was promptly awarded the grant money without having to answer any questions in the native tongue.

As we got older, myself and four of my friends, Sheila Sharkey, Agnes Dan Sharkey, Georganna and Barbara, would entertain the whole island by staging little shows we created ourselves. We even provided the seating using fish boxes and planks of wood. With no radio or television on the island, we always got a full house. Even the priest on the mainland would visit to see our performances, and we were always nervous when he was there for fear of making a mistake in front of him. Everyone revered the priest in those times.

There was one occasion when we decided to do a really elaborate production with lots of costumes, so we headed off on a round of the houses to gather the various items of clothing we thought might suit the scenes and characters we had devised. One sketch required an old-fashioned pair of drawers which went down as far as the knees and had elastic just above them and at the waist. We enquired in all the houses to see if any still existed, but our search was in vain. There was an old lady who lived way up on the mountain, so we headed off to see if by chance she had a pair. We went up to the house and explained our strange request, how we were looking for bloomers that had elastic at the knees. The wee, round lady, with grey hair peeking out from underneath her black headscarf and a face etched with lines, stood in her doorway looking deep in thought.

'Och,' she eventually said, 'I have a pair surely.'

'Could we take a loan of them?' I asked.

'Och,' she replied, 'I couldn't do that. I keep them for the day of the priest.'

Twice a year the priest would come over to the island to do the Stations of the Cross, hear confessions and give out Holy Communion. The old lady only had the one good pair of knickers, so she kept them for those special occasions. Despite our disappointment, we saw the funny side of that situation.

We had good laughs, but there were sad times too. I recall the fear and terrible mourning that swept the island one time when a boat that was fishing herring went up on the rocks and all the fishermen were missing. It had such an impact on the island that I never forgot it. One of the men was from the island, and there were two fishermen from the mainland. My brother James was part of the search party, and it was he who found the body of the Owey man in the sea. He put his boathook into the water in the area where the tragic accident happened, and it caught the poor man's oiled clothing. When they pulled him into the boat, he was dead. The death cast a terrible dark cloud over the entire island for a long time. The sea can be so cruel by times. People spent many more days searching the shore around the island for the other bodies, but they were never found. Fortunately, they were the only fishermen who ever lost their lives on the island in my time.

I went to school on the island up to the age of 14, and that's when my formal education ended. There was no second-level schooling, so from then on you became one of the family earners.

For me, that began even before I left school, when I went into service to a family on the island. I was only 13 at the time, but I was expected to do the work of an adult during my holidays and after school. It was hard labour, and you wouldn't dare complain to anyone about it. I was getting paid for my service, and you got nothing for nothing. And I only got the job because the family knew I was a hard worker.

My service started on St Patrick's Day and didn't come to an end until Hallowe'en. One of the major tasks they set me was to sow the potatoes. I had to dig out the drills with a spade, and that was no easy job. It was like cutting through concrete at times. I had blisters on my hands and my back was aching, but I never gave up. I kept on working my way through the ground from morning until the sun was going down. Eventually I had dug out rows and rows of neat drills. A big, strong farmer would have been hard-pressed to do this job. But even at that age it was a normal job to me. I had always done this kind of yearly work at home. When I prepared the ground, I then planted each of the seed potatoes by hand – rows and rows of them. My whole body ached at the end of each day. When I went to bed at night I went out like a light. The only thing to look forward to at the end of a hard day's work like that was bed.

Next I had to strap two creels over a donkey to manure the potatoes. Digging out the mound of manure was hard work – and stinking – and forking it into the creels nearly crippled me with pain. But I did enjoy working with the donkey because he was a lovely old animal. And, despite what they say about donkeys being thick, he worked well. After filling the creels, I'd take the donkey across to the area where the tatties had been sown. I had to be careful that the donkey didn't trample on the drills, but he seemed to know where to step and where not to. I'd pull the strings of the creels and release all the manure. Then I had to spread the manure across the drills to feed the potatoes and encourage their growth. Finally I'd take the donkey back to the stack of manure and refill the creels. I did that over and over until the job was completed. And I did it all in my bare feet, which meant, of course, that they really stank. I had lots of cuts and scrapes on my feet and legs as well, but, in all honesty, that never bothered me because I was used to it on the island. Reflecting on it today, I don't know how I endured such back-breaking work. The aches in my poor limbs are a constant reminder of those hard times.

It wasn't all bad, though. One of the jobs I really loved was looking after the cattle in the evening up at the mountain. I'd go to check and make sure they were safe and hadn't fallen over a cliff. It was a really peaceful and relaxing time, and I enjoyed the peace and tranquillity up around there.

The turf-cutting, wasn't so easy, however. I'd be sweating in the heat with flies swarming all over me. Some members of the family I was working for would cut the turf and throw it out of the ground, and I would catch it and stack it. This would go on for hours, and it was very, very hard work, especially for a child, never mind the fact that I was a girl.

Later in the year, when the potatoes had grown and were ready to be harvested, it was my job to gather them after they were dug out. I had to do this on my hands and knees, collecting them up into a basket that I pulled along behind me. A pit was dug out of the ground and the tatties were stored there. They were covered with hay to protect them from the winter frost.

I worked right through the summer, and it was a long, hard time. And then in the autumn, I would go to the farm and do the chores immediately after I'd finished school and all over the weekends. At the end of my service, I was handed £2 10s by the family, which was a lot of money in those times. I handed that money over to my mother, and it went towards supporting our family. You'd never dream of keeping any of the money to spend on yourself.

The biggest trauma in my life at that stage occurred when I went into service as a housekeeper after leaving school. The job was with a family in Derry, and it was to be the first time that I would be parted from my mother and father. I was only going on 15, and I was sick at the thought of leaving home.

Although my mother and father had no idea how bad I was feeling, I would cry myself to sleep in the weeks before I left. It was the worst time of my young life. The people I was going to work for were strangers to me, and I had no idea what shocking fate lay in store.

I didn't want to leave home. I didn't want to go and live with strange people. I realized, of course, that there was nothing I could do about it. That's the way it was in those times. You had to go out, make your own way in the world, and support your mother and father, even at that tender age. But knowing that what you were doing was necessary to help your parents make ends meet didn't ease the pain of being separated from them.

I was heartbroken when the time came to leave. I loved Mammy and Daddy and my little island home. I had no idea how long I'd be away or when I'd see my mother and father again. I tried to be strong in front of them, but it was no use. Nothing could stop the flood. I just broke down and sobbed my heart out as I walked away from the house carrying my little case. Glancing back at my mother and father, I could see that they were very upset too. It was heartbreaking for them to see their offspring leaving the nest, heading off into the big world and out of their care and protection.

I sobbed all the way to Derry. I'd never felt so alone. But by the time I reached my destination, I had calmed down a good bit. The man meeting me off the train was called Mr Foley. I was easy to spot on the platform, as I must have looked like a little lost soul standing forlornly with all my worldly possessions in one little case.

'You must be Julia,' said a tall gentleman in a smart suit.

'Yes,' I replied meekly.

'Well, now, let's get you home for a nice up of tea,' he said.

I would soon discover that the Foleys were two of the loveliest people imaginable. The wife was a sister of the bishop of Derry, Dr Farren, and she was partly paralysed from a slight stroke. Her husband was a former policeman. He was so nice that I couldn't imagine him ever arresting anybody. I sensed straight away that Mr and Mrs Foley were a kind and considerate couple, and I wasn't wrong. Within a couple of weeks the pain of separation from my parents went away as I settled into my new regime. And I realized that I had found a home away from home. It was a grand, big house with lots of beautifully carved furniture. Expensive-looking ornaments decorated the rooms. I had been given a lovely, wee room with a very comfortable bed. This was no hardship.

Poor Mrs Foley had lost all of her independence as a result of the stroke, so one of my main responsibilities was to help her with her personal needs. It was very demanding work, but the fact that she was such a nice lady made it easier. I'd assist her to wash and dress every morning before breakfast. Mr Foley would then team up with me, and the two of us would carefully carry her down two flights of stairs. You could see the sadness in Mrs Foley's eyes at the loss of her independence. Yet in all the time I worked for her, I never heard her complain.

The Foleys were a well-to-do family, and all of their children were adults with good jobs. Tommy, Margaret and Molly were teachers, while Jack worked in a chemist's. Everyone in the family had a great sense of humour. The first day I met them, Jack asked, 'Are you able to paint?'

I thought he was being serious, but he was just pulling my leg.

As well as taking care of Mrs Foley, I had to do all the household chores on my own. There were floors to be scrubbed; clothes to be washed by hand and then ironed; sweeping, dusting and, of course, cooking the family meals. But because I felt so loved and appreciated, I did all of my chores with a light heart.

At that time, the local Derry *Journal* was published three times a week – on Monday, Wednesday and Friday. Mrs Foley loved the newspaper and always looked forward to it coming into the house. As she was unable to get out and about, the paper gave her all the news on what was happening out in her locality and the greater county. It provided her with many hours of reading enjoyment. We'd be taking her down the stairs on the morning a new *Journal* was out and Mr Foley would say, 'The Derry rag is here today again.' She'd smile. You could see that they were such a united couple.

Mr Foley was always good-humoured. He was sitting at the breakfast table one morning tucking into the sausages and bacon I had served up. A chunk of a sausage fell off his fork and on to the floor as he was about to eat it. He peered over his glasses and glanced down at the floor. Looking up, he said, 'Do ye know, Julia, you can never be sure of the bite you're puttin' into your mouth.' We all laughed.

There was a big apple tree out in the garden, and when the apples were ripe and ready to be harvested, Mr Foley would climb up on a ladder and shake them down for me to collect. It was idyllic in many ways. They had such a comfortable life compared to the one I'd known back on the island. And they were very rich by our standards. But the Foleys never made me feel inferior.

I went to Mass at 9 a.m. every Sunday with Mr Foley. As Mrs Foley wasn't able to attend church, her brother, the Bishop, would occasionally say a Mass in the house. He came one time while I was out shopping for groceries, and the Mass was over by the time I returned. Just so I wouldn't be upset, Bishop Farren gave me a special blessing. They all treated me like a lady.

Owey and my family were always in my thoughts, though. Every single week I wrote a letter to my mother and father back home, telling them all about my work and the daily happenings in the Foley household. In that way, I felt that I still had my parents in my life. There were no telephones, so I couldn't make contact with them that way. But I knew my letters would be welcomed. I gave them lots of news because this was a new world for me and I had plenty to tell. I'm sure everyone on the island heard all about the goings-on in Derry.

I had other distractions as well. My cousin Bridget Sharkey from home had come to work in Derry, along with a girl called Maggie Gillespie, who was from Kincasslagh. Some evenings for a break I would go down and meet up with them to have a chat. They were great company, and, even though I had settled into the Foley household, I was delighted to have someone to visit while I was in Derry.

After six months with the Foleys, it was time for me to go back to Owey as I was needed to help out with all the spring work around the farm. It took me a long time to pluck up the courage to break the news to Mr and Mrs Foley because I knew they would be upset to see me go. I was performing an important role in their family, and they had also become attached to me on a personal level. However, I didn't realize just how badly they would take the news.

'Ah, Julia, we can't lose you. I'll give you more wages if that will change your mind,' Mr Foley pleaded.

'It's not the money at all, Mr Foley. I really am needed back home to help with the spring work,' I insisted.

'Ah, Julia, you'll not leave us,' Mr Foley begged, and I felt so sorry for him as I could see the look of desperation in his face.

'Mr Foley, sure you'll get some other girl,' I said, trying to reassure him.

Mr Foley began to cry. 'We'll never get another Julia,' he sobbed, cupping his face in his hands. I could see that he was terribly upset.

I had been heartbroken the first day I arrived at the Foleys' to start my job, and I was just as upset the day I was leaving them. The tears ran down my cheeks as I bade them farewell. It cut me to the bone to see them so sad. Two wonderful people, they were. I never forgot them.

Six months was a long time to be away from home, especially as it was the first occasion. It was good for me, though. I had experienced a different kind of life through the Foley family. I had become a bit more confident from having to deal with new people. I had probably grown up a bit. My homesickness had gone away after a few weeks, but as I returned to Owey the excitement started to build up. By the time I reached the island I was ready to explode.

My father was down at the shore to meet me, and he had a big smile on his face.

'God, Julia you're after shooting up. What were they feeding you in Derry?' he laughed.

My mother had the tea ready when I stepped through the door. 'It's lovely to have you back in our wee house,' she said. 'I never missed anyone as much.'

My mother and father missed every one of us when we went away, of course.

James and Edward were away picking potatoes, but Owenie and Maggie were in the house. And they wanted to hear everything about my time with the Foleys.

I was surprised that it took me a few days to settle back on Owey. It was strange at first going back into my old life. And working on the farm again, that was the hardest part. I'd been softened up during my employment with the Foleys because it was housework. It was a lot more genteel. Now I had to become a farmer again.

I remember the first time a radio arrived on Owey – what excitement that caused! A man by the name of John Gallagher, a relative of mine who lived across from our house, was the proud owner of the box, which was fascinating to look at with its knobs and dials. We all watched, adults included, with childish fascination as John switched it on, and it crackled, whistled and hummed as he searched for a station. As he tuned it in and voices came through, we were staring at it in wonderment.

From then on, John's humble cottage was the most visited home on Owey. Everybody made a nightly pilgrimage to the Gallaghers' to hear whatever was on the radio, which had only one station, Radio Eireann. John was an easy-going man who possessed a great sense of humour and was always laughing at something or other. His wife, Peggy, who was a native of Scotland, was equally good-humoured and good-natured; they were a very hospitable couple. Everyone who visited that house was given a cup of tea by Peggy.

We all became addicted to the radio. Later I would enjoy a programme called *The School around the Corner*, which was presented by Paddy Crosbie. It was very funny. Paddy was a tall, skinny Dublin man who always dressed in a smart suit and drew great humour out of the schoolchildren he interviewed. The mind of a child thinks much differently from an adult's, so their responses to Paddy's questions were unpredictable, and sometimes they were hilarious.

I remember how Paddy asked one young lad one night if he had any animals at home.

'We had a horse, sir, but he got sick,' the boy replied.

'And is he better now?' Paddy enquired.

'No, sir,' the boy responded.

'How is he?' Paddy asked.

'He's dead, sir,' said the boy.

'I'm sorry to hear that. And how did he die?' Paddy probed.

'Me father shot him, sir,' replied the boy.

'Shot him?' Paddy said with astonishment.

'Yes, sir. Me father dug a hole and shot him.'

'In the hole?' asked Paddy.

'No, sir, in the head,' replied the boy.

Well, I thought Paddy Crosbie was going to die laughing. It was one of the funniest moments on the show.

The Irish country-music star Maisie McDaniel from Sligo was very popular at that time on the radio as well. We used to tune in to listen to her.

As there was no electricity, the radio was run on a battery, and whenever it ran down John would have to go over to the mainland to get it charged up again. Every household on the island contributed thruppence to this expense because we were all enjoying the entertainment it provided. That was one of the first real gadgets we came across as we crept out of the Dark Ages.

Our own house later became a popular place of entertainment when my father picked up a gramophone cheaply in a market one day, along with some old records. It didn't take long for news of this to spread around the island, and everyone wanted to see and hear this wonderful music machine. Later, when one of the island's teachers, Paddy Kelly, took digs at our house while my brothers were away working in Scotland, he gave my father Bridie Gallagher's first record. Bridie was from Donegal, and she was a big singing star in Ireland.

New inventions gradually made their way onto

the island. There was one old woman who had a frightening experience with a battery-operated flash lamp when they first came out. The house she was visiting had just recently got the lamp, and one night as she was leaving late to go home they gave it to her so that she wouldn't trip and hurt herself in the dark. She was very wary of this strange light but agreed to take it with her. When the little old lady arrived home at her own house, she tried to blow out the light like you would an oil lamp or a candle. She blew and blew, but the light, needless to say, wouldn't go out. Exasperated, the old lady finally gave up trying, and, fearful that it would burn her house down as she slept, she left the lamp sitting outside in a ditch overnight. God bless her innocence.

The people on Owey were very superstitious in those times. There were lots of old wives' tales. If you were dressing in the morning and you happened to put on a cardigan or jumper inside out, you wouldn't dare take it off and turn it right side out because that was said to bring you bad luck. You had to leave it on for the day, and only at night, when you were preparing for bed, could you take it off.

If two teaspoons were accidentally placed on your saucer, it was the sign of a wedding.

You'd be terrified of breaking a mirror because it apparently meant you were going to experience six years of bad luck, and nobody wanted that!

And if it rained on 15 July, folklore said it would then rain for 40 days and 40 nights. Wasn't I born on a bad day!

It was also said that no one ever saw a donkey dying because donkeys are holy animals. They have a cross on the back of their neck. One day our donkey was dying on Owey. I decided to keep a vigil beside my beloved animal as I wanted to be the first person to see a donkey dying. I sat beside the sick pet all day. Eventually I ran into the house for a cup of tea, and when I came out the donkey was dead. And that's a true story!

Any spare moment I'd have at home was spent doing knitting, which I'd mastered as a child, taught by a neighbour called Mary Boyle. I was too young at the start to use needles, as they were considered to be dangerous in the hands of children. Instead, I used feathers from a rooster's wings. My father had honed and shaped them with his pocket knife. Later I graduated to proper needles. At night the women would gather in one house knitting and chatting, while the men would go to a separate house to pass the hours by playing cards and telling yarns. On the way home the men would look at the night sky, and somehow they could predict the weather for the following day. They could tell by the appearance of the sky, the moon and the stars.

When I got older, I discovered the joy of dancing. It became a real passion, even an obsession, to the point where I would deceive my mother and father by pretending that I was going off to houses to knit with some of my friends, when really I was going off dancing with them on the island. On those days, I'd knit as fast as I could while I was away looking after the cows. If I felt that it was less than I'd be expected to achieve at a night's knitting session, I'd stretch the sock to make it look longer. Then I'd hide my handiwork in a hole in the ditch so that my mother wouldn't see it. That night on my way home from my dancing, I'd return to the hole in the ditch, retrieve the woollen sock and then confidently enter the house. If my mother woke up, she wouldn't be bothered as to where I'd been because I had knitting to show for my night's escapade. At other times after the rosary was said at night, and my mother and father had gone to sleep, I'd go out to meet some of the other teenagers to chat and dance. The clock in our house used to strike on the hour every hour, so while my mother and father were sleeping I'd put it back two hours in case they awoke when I was coming in late. Then I'd get up in the morning before them and put it forward again. I didn't see any harm in it as we weren't doing anything untoward.

chapter four

Guttin' and Tattie Howkin'

AS THE PACKED train chugged through the pleasing landscape of Gweedore in the Donegal Gaeltacht, where the native Irish language is spoken, I didn't dare blink for fear of losing sight of Owey.

My heart was full of sorrow and my face a soggy mass from crying as the island became smaller and smaller in the distance.

I let out a big sob as it shrank to a mere dot on the horizon. I was taking the train to the boat, which in turn would take me far away from the island. It would be several months before I'd set foot on Owey again, not until Hallowe'en.

My poor mother and father hadn't been able to conceal their heartbreak as I'd headed down to the currach on the shore. My father would never cry, but I could see in his eyes that he was suffering pain. Three of the family were leaving that day. My older brothers, James and Edward, were travelling with me, as they had got jobs to do with fishing too. My sister, Maggie, and younger brother, Owenie, were the only ones left behind. And Maggie would soon be going off to work in a Scottish hotel.

Emigration, no matter for how short a time, always brought pain to families. It tore loved ones apart in the struggle to survive and put food on the table. After my first experience away in Derry with Mr and Mrs Foley, I thought it wouldn't be such a wrench. But it was much worse. I was now nearly 16 and a new job awaited me at Lerwick, one of the Shetland Islands off Scotland. This time it wasn't housekeeping at the other end of the journey but the daily grind of fish gutting. It was a lovely summer's day in June as I set off, but there was no sunshine in my heart. I was filled with foreboding as I had no notion of what lay in store for me, other than being guaranteed hard work and lots of it.

As the boat journey neared an end, the outline of the houses and the church spire around Lerwick harbour came into view. Lerwick, Shetland's only town and Britain's most northerly one, was a hive of industry at the time thanks to the wealth the herring fishing brought to the local community. One of the community's most notable features was its fine town hall.

I didn't have time to take full stock of my surroundings because I was immediately introduced to my new 'family' – the 'herring girls', as we were known – and given a demonstration of the work that was required. Growing up on an island, I was no stranger to fish gutting, but doing it as part of a team of girls who came from Scotland and many parts of Ireland was a strange, new experience and a lot more demanding. I set about working in a crew of three people, with two of us frantically gutting the fish and the third girl packing them into barrels between layers of coarse salt. As it is an oily fish, herring deteriorates quickly, so it was essential that we swiftly removed the insides with a razor-sharp knife and preserved the fish in the salt. The target was to gut and pack a minimum of 30 barrels a day. Each barrel contained 80 to 100 herring, depending on their size, so you really had to concentrate on getting the job done and there was no slacking off.

As we diligently sliced open the fish and scooped out their insides, we wore oilskin skirts with bibs over our own clothing to save our bodies from the mess of the entrails, the water and the salt. The protective layers of clothes had to be long enough to cover the tops of our boots so as to prevent fish scales and raw pieces of gutted fish slipping down inside our footwear. Our tall rubber boots had wooden soles to cope with greasy surfaces and the corrosive effects of the salt.

Unbleached cotton which came from empty flour sacks was cut into strips, wound round our fingers and fastened with cotton thread in a desperate and mostly useless attempt to protect our hands from the sharp knives and stinging salt. During our dinner break we'd replace the strips, but they were a poor source of protection, and I regularly got excruciating cuts as I went about my business. After a couple of months, my hands looked like they'd been through a bloody battle. The marks of the knife carved out a pattern. Raw wounds were a torture when the coarse salt got into them. I had no choice but to endure the stinging pain and get on with the job. Otherwise I wouldn't get paid.

We did our work out in the open on the quayside in all kinds of weather. The stench from the innards of the fish was often overpowering. This was one of the fishing industry's most gruelling jobs. Our contracts committed us to begin work when required and to continue as long as we wanted; if you put in the extra hours you'd get more pay. We'd normally start at 7 a.m. and finish at 6 p.m., with just a one-hour break for our dinner. In the busiest time you could end up doing 14 or 15 hours and working by lamplight until all the fresh fish had been processed. Standing in the same spot working with the fish at night is hardship I'll never forget.

In particular, the cold I experienced was almost beyond human endurance. The only source of heat was a wee lantern with hot coals in it. Every now and then we'd take turns going to the lantern to warm our hands. But that only made the work harder because once you put your hands into the cold fish again it was torture. At the end of a hard day you'd only be fit for bed. At night we slept in basic wooden huts.

As the weeks wore their way into months, I settled into this tough routine. It's amazing how the human mind and body can adapt and cope with the most difficult of circumstances. But the long-term effects of this work could be seen in some of the older people who suffered from arthritis in their hands caused by working in wet conditions. There were people with chest problems and others affected by sclerosis of the spine from bending into barrels and over fish troughs for long periods.

Owey was never far from my mind while I was working in Lerwick. Every week without fail I would write a letter home to my mother and father, to reassure them that I was safe, healthy and doing just fine. I would never complain about my terrible life. It would have been unfair to trouble my parents, as I'm sure it was a constant worry for them having their children working abroad. They missed us just as much as we pined for them.

James and Edward never wrote a line home, of course. They were men, and it wasn't expected of them. I would always mention them in my letters, saying how they were safe and doing fine at their work. The three of us got on well at work. It was James who took care of the money. Whatever Edward and myself earned we passed on to James. He in turn would post the money home to our mother and father. Although the two boys were older, I adopted the role of mother when we were away. That included washing their stinking work clothes. It was what women did.

After five long months in those conditions, our stint there was over, and, with a light heart, I packed my few bits and pieces, stuffed my final earnings into a sock and headed off to the boat with Edward and James for the journey back home to Owey.

As I stepped out of the currach on the island, I crossed myself in thanksgiving for a safe passage; then my legs took off at a gallop on the short route to our home. It was a thrill to walk through the doorway of our little cottage and see the faces of my mother and father light up with joy at my safe return. In those days families didn't hug and kiss

like they do in these modern times, but you knew by
their body language that there was great love for
you and that they were delighted to have you back
in the house.

Sometime later on Owey, Daddy was struck down
by a severe bout of flu and had to take to his bed. He
was shivering and sweating. He was a very sick
man. My poor mother tended to him with hot drinks
and cool clothes, and I could see that she was
terribly worried about him. At this time Maggie and
the three boys had gone away again to find work, so
it was left to me to do all the chores around the
farm. It was time to harvest the potatoes, and I dug
out and filled 13 barrels with them. There were four
big sacks of potatoes in every barrel. I took them
home on a donkey and put them into a pit and
covered them to protect them from the winter frost.
And I was the first person on the island to have the
potatoes harvested. It was a busy time for me. There
was turf to be brought in and water to be fetched
from the wells. And I milked the cow twice every
day. My poor father felt terribly helpless, but there
was nothing he could do. He'd been raving and
sweating and delirious for several days while going
through the worst of his illness. And it was a relief
to us all when he began to show signs of improve-
ment. It took a couple of weeks for my daddy to get

back on his feet again. When he came to inspect my work, he was so proud of me.

'Y'know, Julia, I don't know what I'd have done without you,' he remarked as he made his way back inside the cottage.

The following year I was back on the chain-gang when I joined a big crew of Owey people, including my brothers James and Edward, for the first of many trips tattie howkin' on the big farms of Scotland. It was June when we set out for our destination, leaving my beloved island and my parents behind. And even though I was travelling with my brothers and many of my neighbours, the homesickness was as bad as ever.

Our destination was Ayrshire in Scotland, and on my arrival at the farm in Kilwinning, where acres of potatoes awaited us, I was shown my sleeping quarters. I now had something in common with the farm animals: we were sharing the cowshed. The pungent smell of hot cow dung and the peculiar odour of the animals which had just been milked was still heavy in the air, even though the area had been washed out with water and swept with yard brushes. As I stared at my spartan new sleeping quarters, I could hardly believe it. I hadn't known what to expect as I'd set out for this land so far removed from Owey, but the cowshed had never been mentioned. It's not that I was accustomed to the finer things in life, but this was as basic as you could get.

'It's certainly no home away from home,' I remarked to Mary, one of the other girls.

'Julia, you'll be so tired you'll be happy to bed down anywhere,' Mary pointed out.

'I suppose you're right,' I replied, as I got set to make up my mattress. Our employer had thrown us some straw, and each of us had to make up our own mattress using bags that had been stitched together. There was a black blanket for every worker and two of us sleeping on one mattress. All the girls slept in one shed, and the men were in a separate one. On the positive side, it was June as I started into this, which took the sting out of having to rough it in these primitive surroundings.

The next morning a lorry arrived for us at 5 a.m., and we all piled onto the back of it. We were like the inmates of a prison camp being driven off to do hard labour. The vehicle was packed with young men and women. We were transported across rough terrain, and the bouncing up and down made me feel sick that first morning. Finally, we reached the fields where we had to reap the tatties. As I jumped down to the ground and walked around to the front of the truck, I glanced across the huge expanse of land that swept before me. There seemed to be no end to the field. It spanned out as far as the eye could see, and I wondered how many weeks I would spend in this field crawling on my hands and knees as I gathered the potatoes.

Tattie howkin' was laborious, painstaking work. It was done by hand at a snail's pace, with the spuds being dug out with three-pronged forks and then collected in baskets. It was back-breaking work, and every day was the same that summer. I'd get to the fields shortly after 5 a.m. and go straight to work. We were under pressure to make as much progress as was humanly possible before the heat of the sun became unbearable. I'd spend hours on my knees, gathering the potatoes into a basket that I pulled along after me. The ground was rock-hard, and as I crawled along through the drills the friction blistered my knees, making the tedious task even harder. My hands were soon decorated with welts and cuts, and clay was caked under my fingernails. Sometimes small, sharp stones would pierce underneath my nails, sending a stinging pain up my fingers and leaving them sore for days. The cuts, punctures and blisters hurt like hell as you worked, and there was never any time for them to heal.

Sometimes the heat in the field was unbearable,

but you couldn't go off to the shade of the trees because there was a job to be done. At 2.00 p.m. the lorry would return to take us back up to the farm where we'd eat and then rest for a time. It was the same routine day in and day out. Later in the year, as the weather changed, we'd go out at 8 a.m. and come home at 5 or 6 p.m. I'd spend hours riddling the potatoes, sorting them and putting them into different bags out in the open. At the end of the week I'd be handed £3 for my labour. It was a small amount of money for such hard work, but that was the going rate, and it was considered to be a good wage. It was either take it or leave it. There was no union fighting for your rights in those days. Whatever money I earned I sent home to my mother and father.

Sometimes after a day in the potato field and a break in the afternoon, we'd go out in the evening to farms to gather up stooks of straw that had been tossed around; you'd make some extra money doing that. You'd spend three or four hours at that work for a wage of half a crown. In the wintertime we'd get extra work in the fish houses, putting fish on skewers. There were two dozen placed on each skewer, and then you'd hand them up to another worker who put them on a rack to dry out before they were taken away to be sold.

When it was time to retire for the night, the stark and smelly cowshed seemed the most welcoming place on earth because I'd be so exhausted from the day's work. The straw bed felt like a deluxe mattress. Mary had been right. I couldn't have cared less where I laid my head down at that stage.

Apart from working on the farm, I also did the cooking and washing for myself and five men: my two brothers, James and Edward, the gaffer and two other men. There was no pay for that. I was a woman and that's what was expected of women. I never questioned it. It's just the way it was.

We moved from farm to farm during the potato-picking season. Even though you'd think there was no end to a field, you'd always get there. Then you'd move on to the next job.

They were the harshest of times, but somehow we always brought some fun into our lives. When you're young you crave music and dancing, and at week-ends that was what we sought out. You'd walk for miles to a local dance, and sometimes you'd be barely home when you'd have to get up again and go to work in the fields. We were all young, and you're full of energy and game for any kind of adventure at that time of your life. We didn't have much money for our own entertainment as whatever we earned was sent home to the island. We kept just enough for essential needs and a little bit for entertainment. It cost thruppence to get into the dances in those times. I only had a couple of shillings to spend in a week. I might spend some of it on a paper, but mostly I bought wee biscuits or sweets: I loved sweets at that time.

God forgive me, but I remember how one time when the weekend came round I discovered that I hadn't kept back enough money to go dancing. I couldn't go to James and ask him for more money because I knew that he'd give me a telling off for spending my weekly ration. Instead, I sifted through his clothes and found sixpence in one of his pockets. So, God forgive me again, I stole the sixpence from him. James knew that his sixpence had gone missing, but he didn't know who took it and I never told him. You'd get a lot for sixpence at that time. A loaf of bread would hardly cost you sixpence then. A box of matches was only a ha'penny.

Throughout my late teens and into my 20s, that was the pattern of my life: leaving Owey for months at a time to work at the fish gutting or tattie howkin'. In his house on Owey a distant cousin of mine called Jim McGinty would often recite a poem he'd written about fish gutting in Lerwick:

It's the start of the summer and the boys going
   away
To work at the turnips, the harvest and hay
To go to the guttin' I'd made up my mind
Tho' my heart it was sore for the folks left behind
When we landed in Lerwick it sure was a sight
Our foreman was there he was full of delight
To see all his gutters arrive back once more
To the old town of Lerwick and Shetland's green
   shore
After some greeting and a great deal of fuss
The foreman conveyed us to Ganson's wee bus
We all started off for our new abode
God knows it was dreary the grimest of road
We got cooking utensils we got pieces for cloots
We got oilskins and aprons and short rubber boots
The gutters got knives and packers got scoops
And the whole thing was tallied in the foreman's
   notebook
At half-five the next morning the foreman came
   round
He knocked at the window from within came no
   sound
When no one made answer it filled him with rage
And he shouted right back, 'You'll get no weekly
   wage'
At last came the day the fishing was o'er

Once more we were leaving Shetland's green shore
With the fondest of memories we'll always recall
The dances we had in Donaldson's hall
So good-bye to you Lerwick and Bressay also
For it's back to old Ireland I'm planning to go
But I hope that some day I'll come back o'er the
   sea
If the Lord has allowed me a gutter to be.

Jim is 90 years old as I write, and he can still recite this wonderful poem from our time in Lerwick. And, like myself, Jim's fondest memories of Lerwick are the great dances we enjoyed there.

During one of my terms in Scotland there was a big gang of potato-pickers from Donegal and Mayo on the same job. The main sleeping area that had been arranged for the workers couldn't accommodate the exceptionally large crew, so they put six of us girls into a different shed on the farm. It was clean inside and we found nothing to complain about; not that you would anyway, as no one would listen to you. There were shelves along the walls containing lots of empty jam pots that were in storage. We made up our makeshift beds and settled down. In the middle of the night our sleep was disturbed by the clinking sound of the jam jars striking off each other.

'Do you hear that? What's that?' Kathleen, one of the girls, shouted out in the dark.

'Lord save us, is this place haunted?' someone whispered as jam jars came crashing onto the floor.

Maura, another of the girls, struck a match, and someone let out a piercing scream.

In the dimly lit room I could see the cause of her terror; the place was crawling with rats. Well, we were out of there like lightning, roaring our heads off as we ran for dear life across the farmyard to the shed where the rest of the female crew were bedded down for the night.

Despite the work being hard, the people we worked for weren't demons. Our accommodation certainly left a lot to be desired and wouldn't be tolerated in modern times, but there was no one shouting at you while you worked. We were all supplied with free milk and potatoes, fuel and light as part of our deal. And I encountered some very nice people.

One evening I was down getting milk at the home of the ploughman on the Scottish farm where we were working at the time. The ploughman's wife was a plump lady with a big smile and an easy laugh. She kept her house lovely. It was like a doll's house with lots of pretty ornaments, including two dogs that stood on guard each side of the fireplace.

'God, aren't they lovely,' I said to her one day.

'Do you like them?' she responded.

'I do,' I said.

The fields on this farm were enormous. Three weeks later I was still there picking the potatoes when there came a message for me that I was wanted down in the ploughman's house. I was very worried then, thinking that I must have done something wrong. When I went down, it was the ploughman's wife who came to greet me at the door of the cottage. She invited me in.

'You like them dogs, don't you?' she said.

'Well, I just think they are lovely,' I replied.

'They were a wedding present when we got married and I'd like you to have them now,' the ploughman's wife said.

'Och, I couldn't take them,' I said, even though my heart was racing at the thought of getting them as a present.

'No, Julia, I'd love you to have them for your own home when you marry,' the kind woman insisted.

I was beaming from ear to ear as I left her house that evening with those ornamental dogs. The woman had carefully wrapped them in newspaper and put them into a small sack. I was so excited as I made my way back to our humble lodgings that you'd swear I was carrying a bag of gold. Those porcelain dogs were a wonderful gift, particularly as they were of such sentimental value to the lady of that house. Why she gave them to me I'll never know, but I have always treasured them. To this day they are proudly displayed on my own mantlepiece.

As time went on I was able to save money from my allowance during working trips away in Scotland to buy presents for my mother and father. I'd sift through the second-hand shops for bargains, and I was very skilled at finding bits and pieces that I knew my parents would appreciate. I'd never buy anything that they would consider to be extravagant or a waste of money because that would have been frowned upon during those hard times.

I recall one day going into a second-hand shop and spending a lot of time rummaging through the hangers and shelves without any success.

'There's more stuff out the back if you have the time to take a look,' the shop owner told me.

'I've all the time in the world today,' I told him.

It was dark out the back, but I could see lots of clothes at the end of the room. As I walked across the floor, I suddenly fell through a trap-door. I thought I was going to be killed as I hit the ground with a loud thud. Fortunately, the only damage was to my dignity. When he heard the commotion, the man came running to see what had happened.

'I'm all right,' I said, as I picked myself up and dusted myself down. It was the blessing of God that saved me from being killed.

'Dammit, I didn't know that was left open,' the owner said. 'I'll tell you what, young woman, pick out something for yourself and I'll give you a good deal.'

It was then I spotted a cardigan that I knew my mother would love.

'How much is that cardigan?' I asked the shop owner.

'A shilling to you,' he said with a smile.

It was a bargain, and I bought it on the spot. I was delighted with my purchase, but I needed something to give my father as well. I explained this to the man, who said that he had some good-quality jackets that had come in a few days earlier. They weren't out on view, but if I cared to sift through the boxes I was welcome.

I came out smiling with a jacket that cost me only 1s 6d. Never mind my pride, I thought. Sometimes good things can come out of a fall.

When I returned to the island at the end of the working season, my mother and father were delighted with their gifts. From then on, the cardigan and the jacket became 'good wear', only put on for show when the priest came to the island to do the Stations of the Cross. My mother had that cardigan until the day she died, and then I wore it after her!

Don't ask me how she did it, but my sister, Margaret, escaped the hard labour that I went through. Margaret had to leave the island, of course, to find work, so she didn't avoid that heartbreak. Coming up to the age of 16, she migrated to Glasgow where she immediately got a job as a waitress in the George Hotel. Like the rest of us, whatever money Margaret had left out of her earnings, after covering her living expenses, she sent home to our mother and father on the island every month. Although the work was easier than mine, it was still a hard life for her. Margaret was on her own in Glasgow. The digs where she was staying with some of the other hotel workers were very grim, and terribly cold in the wintertime. However, moving to Glasgow would eventually change the course of her life.

It was in Glasgow during the war that she met and fell in love with a small, stocky but good-looking young American man called Bill Chancellor, who was in the navy and was stationed in Scotland at the time. After a whirlwind romance, Margaret and Bill married in June 1945. None of the family made it over for the wedding, as we couldn't afford the expense of the trip. But Margaret had the blessing of our mother and father.

Margaret and Bill were parted the following year when he returned to the States with his ship. Later, she was among the excited young women on a liner carrying what were known as the 'GI brides' to America. When she eventually landed in New York, Bill was there to meet her. Margaret was one of the lucky ones. Some unfortunate brides found themselves all alone in a foreign land after their ships docked. Their husbands seemed to have forgotten while they were overseas that they already had wives back in America. Later, Bill went to work in the oil business, and he and Maggie had three children. Bill did well, and the family were able to afford to travel back to Ireland to holiday on Owey. That was always an occasion of great excitement, not just for our family but for the entire island. Whenever 'the Yankees' were coming, everyone on Owey would join in the party.

Bill was a lovely man. Everyone in the family was very fond of him. Sadly, he too has passed to the next life.

chapter five

Francie

T HERE COMES A time in every young woman's life when she yearns for love and romance. In the circle of life, she has her dreams of becoming a wife and a mother, and of making a home of her own. I was no exception. When I reached my 20s, I wanted that fairy tale too. Little did I know, as I took my first steps along the path, that as well as the joy that love brings, it can also cause terrible pain. The sweet and sour of love were things I would soon discover.

Here I have to state that I feel it would be unfair of me to reveal the identify of a young man who caused me heartache and grief during that early period in my life. It was all so long ago, he is no longer with us on this earth, and I have no intention of hurting any soul, living or dead, in this book. But it would also be unfair to the reader to withhold such a personal trauma. It's one of the blows in life that shaped me as a person. It's through setbacks that you learn how to deal with the hard knocks.

They make you wiser and stronger, and they make you appreciate the good things and the great people who wander through your life. So I'll tell my story while protecting the name of my boyfriend.

It had started out as an ordinary day on Owey. I woke up in the morning full of joy. I was home again on the island after another term of tattie howkin' in Scotland. It was always such a great feeling to be back with my mother and father and my siblings in familiar surroundings. I slipped easily into the routine that involved attending to the various jobs that came my way. Now in my 20s, I was also enjoying the social activities on the island with people my own age. In particular I was looking forward to the local dance.

There was a ruggedly handsome young man on the island who had taken my fancy. He was tall with lovely green eyes and a mop of brown, curly hair. He had a great smile, and he made me laugh whenever we met when we were out and about around Owey. There was no one else at the time that I was interested in. This was the young man I now dearly wanted. We had grown up together so there was nothing, I felt, that I didn't know about him. Funnily, I hadn't thought of him as a prospective suitor in my early teens. Then one day I suddenly became aware that I was attracted to him. It was like being struck by Cupid's arrow, and I became smitten. Every day he was in my thoughts, and I wondered if he felt the same way.

One day I met him by chance as he cycled along an island path. We made small talk, chatting about the weather and other tittle-tattle of little consequence. And then he asked me if I was going to the dance in the hall. My heart began to flutter as I told him that I'd be there.

'See you there, then, and I'll dance with you,' he replied with a wink. Then he threw his leg over the bicycle and pedalled off into the distance.

I couldn't wait for the dance to come round. I just sensed that something was going to happen between us. And I wasn't disappointed.

We danced together all that night.

'Do you want to go out with me, Julia?' he asked afterwards.

'Well, I'd like nothing better,' I replied.

We both smiled, and there was an easy silence between us. I think we were both relieved that we had finally got together. Obviously he had been interested in me for some time too. I now had a boyfriend, and he had a girlfriend. And in the blink of an eye it seemed the whole island knew about it. There were no secrets on Owey, at least not for long.

From that moment we became a courting couple.

I was so happy. Every morning, in the months that followed, when I'd wake up he was the first person I thought of. Soon, in my mind, I was making plans for our future together. I thought I'd found the man of my dreams. I thought this man was going to make a fine husband. We even talked about marriage, and he was keen. I had a skip in my step I was so happy. He was a good catch, or so I thought. Little did I know the heartache that lay around the corner.

One day as I herded the cows along the path to the mountain, I truly didn't have a care in the world. My life was going in a direction that I was very happy with. I began to daydream about the future with my man. It was still early days in the relationship, but I was looking forward to becoming a wife sooner rather than later. I loved children and was living for the day when I would become a mother myself. Like all my friends, I was excited about raising my own little ones, and happily it seemed I wouldn't have to wait many more years. I was in love for the first time in my life.

Suddenly I was jolted out of my thoughts by a familiar figure on a bicycle. It was a young man who was a cousin of my boyfriend. From his facial expression I could see that he was none too happy about something. I had always been quite friendly

My little piece of heaven on earth. These views of beautiful Owey Island bring joy to my heart. My island home (centre) is derelict now, which saddens me.

My parents James and
Margaret McGonagle,
pictured in 1959.

Here I am, aged 17,
(back row extreme
right) with the tattie
howkin' girls in Scotland.

While sifting through a box of old photographs for my book, I found this rare portrait taken in my early 20s. Little did I know then where life was going to take me.

I was the happiest woman in the world when Francie O'Donnell came into my life. He was a fine, handsome man, and here we are pictured together in 1948, the year we were married.

I often stop to realize
That I'm a lucky man,
For when we two were married, dear,
My happiness began...
That's why your every happiness
Is all I'm hoping for
And why each Christmastime we share
I love you more and more!
From Francie to Julia
with love
x x x x x

A treasured Christmas greeting from Francie.

With my baby daughter, Margaret, at my parents' house on Owey.

Happy times with Francie and our children John Bosco and Margaret.

My youngest son, Daniel, aged 1.

Bathing my baby daughter Margaret. There were no
mod cons in those days!

John Bosco grew up to be a strong and healthy child, despite being born prematurely.

A smartly dressed John Bosco on the day of his First Communion, with Kathleen and Margaret.

Daniel, aged 7, on the day of his First Communion in 1968.

A visit to Francie's grave on the day of Daniel's Confirmation in 1972.

with this fellow and wondered if I had done something to offend him. His forehead was creased by a troubled frown, and he appeared to be slightly nervous as he approached me.

He beckoned me over. Whatever had I done?

'What's up?' I asked.

There was an uneasy silence that seemed to last for an eternity. Now I was beginning to be overcome by a feeling of nervousness.

'I have something to tell you,' he finally said, removing his cap.

My heart started to pound. Had something terrible happened to my boyfriend? I looked into his eyes for some sign of what was troubling him.

Then he said the words no girlfriend or wife ever wants to hear. He told me that my boyfriend was seeing another girl behind my back.

At first the words rolled round in my brain and it was a few seconds before they struck home to my heart. I must have gone into shock for an instant, and I had to ask him to repeat what he had just told me.

'I'm sorry, Julia,' he added, when he told me what he had come to say to me. 'I thought you should know.' With that, he got on his bike and cycled off across the island. I was frozen to the spot as the humiliation of what he'd revealed to me sunk in. Then I broke down and sobbed my heart out, barely able to catch my breath amid fits of crying. I couldn't believe that the young man I adored could treat me so cruelly. I had loved that fellow with all my heart, and I'd never looked at another young man from the time that we started going out together.

The rest of that day went by in a blur. The floodgates had opened, and I just cried and cried. I had endured physical pain all my working life, but it was nothing compared to the emotional trauma I was experiencing. 'How could he do it to me?' I asked myself over and over again.

Up on the mountain I sat on a rock and cried my eyes out till the evening, when it was time to return to my home. I was in a terrible emotional state, and then I began to worry about having to face my family. There was no disguising my upset. Upon my return, I slipped into the house and quickly washed my face. If anyone had noticed that something was amiss with me, they said nothing.

Later in the evening I saw my boyfriend going off on his bicycle. He had land over by the strand on the opposite side to where I lived with my family. I spotted him from the window of our barn and decided to follow him secretly. He went off in his currach, no doubt to see the other girl on the mainland. I broke down and cried again, my stomach churning at the thought of him with someone else.

Later, I watched him return. Little did he know the pain he was inflicting on me. I was in floods of tears, but I didn't go to confront him on the spot. I wasn't in any fit state to face him.

When we did meet, after he called round to see me the following day, I was more composed, though still very upset. By the look on his face, I knew he didn't know what was the cause of my troubled state. I wasn't long about telling him. I told him that I knew he'd been cheating on me with another girl and that I didn't want anything more to do with him. He didn't protest. The guilt on his face said it all as he turned on his heel and walked away. Again, my emotions came spilling out in the form of tears.

They say that time heals all wounds, including heartbreak. I did come to terms with the betrayal and the loss; eventually, after a few months, the pain eased a good bit. The pain goes, but you never forget the hurt. It's not something I would wish on any person.

There's an expression: 'What goes around, comes around.' Several months later I heard that my ex-boyfriend had split up with his girlfriend on the mainland. Apparently he went over to meet her one evening and caught her with another man. As hard as it is to believe, he then had the gall to come to my door and ask me to go out with him again.

After the suffering he had put me through, he got an ice-cold reception from me. This time I wasn't upset, just red in the face with rage. He had an awful cheek thinking that I would welcome him back. 'I'm no better today than the day you left me for the other one,' I told him as I closed the door and shut him out of my life.

Judging by the look on his face, I knew he was feeling like a fool. Sending him off with his tail between his legs didn't make me feel any better about what had been done to me. There was no winner in that situation. The only good thing that came out of it for me was the relief that I hadn't married this person. And the dream of marriage and children was still there for another day. Somewhere out there was another man I could share my life with. I was sure of that. After all, I was still a young woman.

When I joined the fish-gutting crew in Lerwick at the start of the following summer, I had no inkling of what fate had in store for me, other than steady employment for a few months. I certainly never suspected that my life would change for ever.

At work one day, as I slit open a herring, one of the other girls started chatting about a Saturday-night dance. It was going to be held down in one of the big huts, known as 'the Rest'. That kind of news was always guaranteed to lift my spirits: I lived for the joy of dancing at the time. It was the excitement of dancing itself, more than the men, that attracted me. As I washed and changed my clothes that night before making my way to the hut with a gang of the girls, the thought of romance wasn't at the forefront of my mind. I was just looking forward to having a good time. On those occasions we'd dance into the early hours, putting all our cares behind us for the evening.

That night the hut was packed with all of the men and women who were working at the fishing, and there was a great atmosphere. The musicians were in full flow when I arrived, not that they were a big band. Two men with a tin whistle and a mouth organ were providing the music to dance to.

Among the crowd I noticed a tall and very handsome young man who had lovely brown hair with a wave through it. He was looking at me from across the room. It struck me that he had a strong physique and a great smile. I had seen this young man before, but something about him that night caught my interest. As I was thinking what a fine man he was, he came over and asked me to dance. He's very good-looking, I thought to myself as we kicked up our heels on the floor among all the other dancers. He told me his name was Francie O'Donnell. We danced a couple of times throughout the night, and I realized that this young man was paying me a lot of attention. Now I was really interested. We'd part after the different sets, and sometimes we'd dance with other people. Late into the evening, instead of taking me up again, Francie asked another girl to dance and I wasn't too happy about that. I suppose, if the truth was known, I became jealous that he was showing attention to another young woman. I left the dance and headed off up the road to my hut, which wasn't very far from the Rest.

When I was halfway there, I happened to turn around and look back. Francie was running up the road behind me. I pretended that I didn't want to be caught and took off at a gallop myself. As I reached the top of the hill, there was a roll of barbed wire in my path, and I fell as I tried to avoid it. Francie came up, caught me … and it was there and then that we shared our first kiss. I knew from that moment that Francie O'Donnell was the man for me. I'm not sure how we know these things. There's an instinct that tells you. The butterflies in my stomach were also a good indication. Francie left me at the door of my hut that night, and as we parted he said, 'I'll come up and see you tomorrow night.' From that moment on, Francie O'Donnell was my man.

When I reflect on it, we were obviously destined to be together. Francie came from Acres near Burtonport, which was on the mainland and in the vicinity of Owey Island. Yet I'd never laid eyes on him until we were both on the fishing crew at Lerwick in the Shetlands. I suppose it doesn't matter what path you take to the one you love as long as you meet up at a crossroads somewhere along the way.

After the dance in the hut, Francie and I became a couple, and I lived for the evenings when he'd come up to meet me. He'd be going out to farms to buy eggs, and he'd ask me to go with him. It may seem strange to people today, but we actually only spent a month together when we first met because it was coming towards the end of our work in Lerwick. But we both knew very soon that we wanted to be together for the rest of our lives. People didn't hang about in those times. We got to know each other very quickly. It helped, I suppose, that we were from similar backgrounds. I was familiar with the area in County Donegal where he'd grown up. During the remainder of our time in Lerwick, we'd go for long walks in the evening and sit and chat for a couple of hours. I told him all about my life growing up on the island. He told me about his background and the places he'd worked. Francie was a fine man and a good man. After my first experience of men, I had been cautious about a new relationship, but somehow with Francie I just knew he'd never let me down.

By then, Hollywood had arrived in Lerwick, and we would occasionally go to the pictures. One night as we were going in, we met another couple from back home by the name of Paddy Bonnar and Mary Gallagher, who were from Belcruit. They had let it be known that it wouldn't be long before they'd be getting married.

'I suppose you'll be going over to Belcruit when you go home to ask Paddy Gallagher for a cow and half of his manure,' Francie joked with Paddy Bonnar.

Paddy laughed at the suggestion that he'd be looking for a dowry when he married Mary. Francie was always joking and having a laugh.

All too soon, however, the time came for us to part. Francie was going on to another job pulling beet in Barrow-on-Furness in Scotland, while I was going home to the island. It was the first time that I had sadness in my heart returning to Owey.

During the next couple of months, we continued our courtship by letter. We missed each other terribly, so every letter we received was treasured. They would always end with the line 'Looking forward to seeing you.' Later that winter we were reunited, this time in Yarmouth. It was so wonderful to be in Francie's company again. I just loved being with him. It's not that we were having a great life, because we both had to cope with very hard work in all weathers. There was nothing romantic about it, but we were just happy to be around each other. And the more time I spent with him, the more I saw his inner strength and his goodness.

Francie, I could see, was a very religious man. He was a devout Catholic. He'd never miss Mass on a Sunday. Prayer was an important part of his life. He was serious about his religion and his work, but he was light-hearted too, and he made me laugh. He had everything I could have wished for in a man, including good looks. He was very athletic-looking at that time. So when Francie asked me to marry him during that period together, I had no hesitation in saying yes.

'Are you happy enough to marry me?' Francie had asked.

'I am surely,' I replied with obvious delight.

When that fishing work came to an end for us, I went back home and he went to work on a Scottish farm. Once again our only contact was through letter-writing. Every week we spent apart made me realize just how much I wanted Francie in my life. The next time we saw each other was in June of the following year, when we were both back at the fishing work on a three months' stint. Now we both had something to look forward to at the end of it. We had decided that we would wed on 22 September. I was the last in our family to marry. James had married his girlfriend, Peggy. Margaret, as I mentioned, married Bill. Edward married Mary, and Owenie married Muriel. (Edward's wife Mary died and some years later he married Alice).

My wedding day was the most exciting and emotional of my young life. The year was 1947. I was 28 years old, while Francie was a year younger. I suppose if it had been today they'd be calling him my 'toy boy'. But toy boys hadn't been invented then. Just a couple of weeks earlier, Francie and myself had gone off together to buy the ring. There was no big excursion down to Dublin to go browsing in some of the fancy jewellery stores there. Instead, the two of us went up to the local chemist's shop in Dungloe and picked out a ring. It was a very simple gold band. Although he was by my side at the time, like most men Francie took a back seat when I was making my selection. Once I was happy, that's all that mattered as far as he was concerned. Oh, I wouldn't have been more excited if the ring had come from Tiffany's. Back home on the island, every day in the run-up to the wedding I'd open the box just to have a look at it. It gave me such a thrill. I so loved that ring.

Although my mother and father had never met Francie – and wouldn't do so until the day of the wedding – they were both very happy to see me getting married. I suppose they accepted that their work had been done and they were glad to see me settling down. Seeing a daughter married off was a great relief for most parents in those times. 'Well, God bless you, and the best of luck' is what my father said to me when I broke the news to them.

On the eve of my wedding, I packed a small case and prepared to leave Owey. I was going to stay with my cousin, Bridget Sharkey, over on the mainland in case a storm blew up overnight and prevented me from getting to the church on time the following morning. My excitement over the wedding was tinged with sadness. I was leaving my mother and father and flying the nest to start the next chapter in my life. Despite the harshness of life on Owey, I had loved living there. And my mother and father had meant everything to me. I would still see them, of course, but now I was about to make my own way in the world as a wife and, if God granted me the gift, as a mother.

I was upset as I bid farewell to Mammy. Daddy was over by the school mending fishing nets.

'Go over now and say good-bye to your father,' my mother said to me.

I went over to my father, and we talked about the progress he was making with his work.

'You'll be marrying in the morning,' Daddy remarked as he fiddled with the net.

'I will,' I said. 'I'm off now.'

I just couldn't bring myself to say the word good-bye.

My cousin was all excited to see me. She was playing a big role in my wedding. As Margaret had emigrated to America, I had asked Bridget to be my bridesmaid. Bridget was a dressmaker, and she had made my wedding outfit. It was a lovely blue, two-piece suit – a jacket and skirt – and she'd got me a little navy hat to match. Bridget and myself chatted that night for a couple of hours while drinking cocoa. We were reminiscing about our youth, and the time I'd spent in Derry with the Foleys when I'd gone to visit her sometimes in the evenings. Eventually it was time to go to bed. With all the excitement, I thought I'd never close my eyes that night. Despite this, I slept soundly.

The next day I awoke early, around 6 a.m., and got up and made myself a cup of tea. It was a lovely September dawn. There was still a hint of summer in the air and no sign of the leaves departing the trees. Bridget came out of her bedroom with a smile on her face. 'Looks like you're going to have good weather for your big day,' she remarked. Indeed, it looked like the sun was going to split the stones. The wedding ceremony had been set for 11 a.m. and I waited until the last moment before putting on my lovely new suit as I didn't want anything to spoil it.

There were twenty guests, including family members, and just four motor-cars at the wedding. Neither Francie's widowed mother nor my mother and father were there for my big occasion. That wasn't unusual in those times. The older people often didn't go to weddings. Francie's mother was looking after her grandchildren, as his brothers and sisters were at the wedding.

When I arrived, Francie and his best man – his older brother, Dinny, whom I'd only met once very briefly when we were in Scotland – were already waiting at the altar. When I reached that spot and turned to Francie, he looked like a prince to me in his dark suit and white shirt with blue tie. I could see that he was a little nervous, but he was still smiling. I was nervous too, standing there in front of the local priest, but it was a very quick ceremony. 'I now pronounce you man and wife,' the priest said at the end. And that was it. I was now Julia O'Donnell. It was a simple affair with no music or flowers, and no photographer to capture that special moment in our lives. At the end of the Mass, as we filed out of the church and into the sunlight, the men lit up their cigarettes, and one by one they came and shook hands with us. The women, all dressed in their Sunday best, hugged me and shook Francie's hand. 'The best of luck now,' I heard ringing in my ears as we left the grounds of the little country church.

Francie and I got into the back seat of one of the cars, and we were driven the short journey to Campbell's Hotel in Dungloe for breakfast. The entire wedding party followed, and we all sat around a big table, tucking into bacon, egg and sausage. A big fry-up sealed the marriage. I remember how the bill was £2 12s 6d!

But the wedding celebrations were just starting. We sat around chatting for the remainder of the morning. Then we were off again, this time to the village of Dunfanaghey, where we had lunch in a local hotel. We were really pushing the boat out.

Later in the evening we returned to Logue's pub in Kincasslagh. Little did I know what awaited me. The wedding festivities were just starting in earnest. My father and two other men were down at the pier and standing by a boat, waiting to take us back to Owey.

'That's my father,' I said to Francie when I spotted him. 'I hope everything is all right back on the island. C'mon over and meet him.'

It was the first time for those two great men in my life to meet.

'You got a good girl, there,' my father remarked to Francie as they shook hands.

'Indeed I know it,' Francie replied.

There wasn't an awkward moment between the two of them. Both were very relaxed in each other's company. I knew that my father would like Francie. You couldn't not like Francie, it's just the kind of man he was.

It was 9 p.m. when we arrived on the island, and Francie and myself went straight to my family home. There was a big meal laid on for us – as if we needed more food with the day we'd just had! – but it was lovely to see everyone so excited and making a fuss over us. My mother was delighted to finally meet the man I'd never stopped talking about when

I was at home on the island. I could see that she too was charmed by him. 'He's a lovely man,' she whispered to me amid the commotion in the house.

Afterwards, we went over to the school, where all the islanders who were able to walk had gathered for a night of music and dance. There was poteen being handed around, and soon everyone was in high spirits. Inside, the schoolhouse was lit up with the tilley lamps from the island homes, and soon chalk was rising from the floor as the dancing got into full swing. Francie and myself were the first to take to the floor to great cheering from those gathered round us.

I never doubted for a moment that everyone would like Francie. And I was right. He impressed all the islanders that night. All my family and neighbours on Owey assured me during the celebrations what a fine catch he was.

'You got a good man there, Julia,' one woman remarked.

'I know it well. God blessed me,' I replied.

All through the night the compliments were flying. Every one of the islanders had a great welcome for Francie, and he was the life and soul of the party. He had a lovely singing voice and could play the flute as well. The dancing and singing continued until the sun came up, with Francie and myself in great demand out on the floor. Everyone wanted to have a dance with the bride and groom. It was one of the best wedding parties ever on Owey, even if I say so myself. I was wishing the celebrations could just go on and on. It was morning when we finally got to bed. We stayed in my family home. Francie and myself were in my room, with James and Edward next door. It had been a long day and night, and we fell asleep in each other's arms.

The following day we headed off to Francie's family home, which was my first visit there. It was also the first time I met his mother. Her husband had died five years earlier from cancer. Francie was one of eight boys, including twins, and I got a great welcome in that house from their mother. Oh, she was a lovely woman. 'I hope the pair of you will enjoy a long and happy life together,' she whispered in my ear as she hugged me. We stayed in the O'Donnell house overnight, and then the following day we returned to Owey, where all the excitement had died down and it was back to normal day-to-day living.

Even though we were still on our honeymoon, Francie and I had to chip in and lend a hand with the farm work. Within a few hours back on the island, I was out in my bare feet and on my hands and knees in the clay gathering the potatoes that Francie and my father were digging out with two spades. We spent the rest of the week doing that job. That was our honeymoon.

After just a week together on Owey it was time to go out and earn our living. And, in what was to become the pattern of our married life, we were immediately separated. Francie had got a job in Scotland pulling beet on farms, while I joined a local crew who were off to Great Yarmouth on the north Norfolk coast in England to pack herring. It would be Christmas before I saw my husband again.

I was heartbroken to be leaving Francie so soon into our marriage, and I pined for him every day that I was away. It didn't help that I was doing hard labour in atrocious conditions. The work in Yarmouth was out in the open, and we had to put our heads down and do the job in driving wind and rain. There was little or no thought for the welfare of the workers. Nothing mattered except the fish being gutted and processed as fast as possible. The squawks of the seagulls that circled above the harbour were drowned out by the noise of the fishermen as they hoisted their baskets onto the quay, where all of us workers struggled to keep up with the hundreds of thousands of herring coming in each day.

But while our job was tough, the poor fishermen's

was a lot worse, and far more dangerous. They could be at sea for weeks, struggling for dear life through storms and spending up to five hours at a time on deck hauling in the nets. Our earnings, of course, never reflected the long hours and the hardship we all had to endure. As always, it was someone else up the line who was reaping the rich rewards of our hard labour. The people turning over the money in Yarmouth were the wealthy merchants. The cramped rows where we lived were in the shadow of their houses. From their vantage point, the well-off could look out at the hive of industry below them and watch their money mount up. I doubt if they ever gave us a second thought.

After a couple of months working in those terrible conditions, I got a reprieve when my sister-in-law Muriel, Owen's wife, asked me to come up to their home in Dundee in Scotland and take over the house-work while she went into hospital to have her first child. My brother James was working in Dundee and living with them at the time, so I had to go and look after the two men. I stayed on to help after Muriel arrived home with her little bundle of joy, a boy also called James, who today has a wife and family of his own. I was reunited with Francie in Dundee that Christmas, for the first time since we'd been parted just a week into our marriage. It was a lovely reunion. I was so happy to have him with me. I always said I didn't care where I lived as long as I had my lovely husband with me. It's just that the struggle to survive didn't allow us to be together.

My happiness didn't last long as the search for work separated us again shortly after Christmas. Francie returned to Scotland, and I went back to the quay in Yarmouth. We were struggling to provide for our future, and the little money we were making was all going into the one purse, his and mine.

One day a letter arrived in Yarmouth for me. It was from my mother, and she wrote that I was wanted back home. My brother James's wife, Peggy, had had her first baby, a daughter called Margaret. My mother wrote how Peggy had developed a blood clot in her leg – they called it 'white leg' – and she was going to be in bed for the best part of a year. She had to keep her foot in a lobster pot to avoid movement because the clot could go to her brain. I was needed back home to look after baby Margaret. I folded the letter, stuffed it in my pocket and made immediate plans to return. Back home, it was a very busy time for me. I was milking the cow and doing all the washing and baking and cooking. My mother had a sore knee, and I was looking after her, helping her in and out of bed.

As the months passed, Peggy recovered and

Margaret blossomed into a fine, healthy child. She is also married today with children of her own. But as Peggy was recovering, I was being very foolish, even reckless, about my own health – as I was about to discover.

chapter six

John Bosco and the Shoe Box

FRANCIE WAS DELIGHTED when I wrote and told him my news: we had a baby on the way. Now we were going to be a real family. Like every woman, I regarded the prospect of becoming a mother as the greatest gift from God. Each day I prayed that we would be blessed with a healthy child. And Francie told me in his letters that he was praying for me too. In the latter stages of pregnancy I really needed the benefit of those prayers because I became very ill.

My poor mother took a bad turn around that time, and we all feared the worst. She looked for all the world like she was at death's door. My brother Owen and his wife, Muriel, came over from Dundee to see her. Muriel took one look at me as she came through the door, and I could see by her expression that she was shocked.

'Are you not well yourself, Julia?' she asked.

'I'm not myself, but sure I'm pregnant,' I said.

'Oh, Julia, being pregnant is not an illness, and

you don't look very well to me,' Muriel replied, and I could hear the concern in her tone.

I didn't know there was anything wrong with me. I didn't feel great, but I'd put it down to my condition. After all, I was seven months gone at the time.

'Your face is swollen, Julia. I think you should see the doctor,' Muriel advised.

'Ah, I'll be just fine when I get a rest,' I protested. When you're young you think you can fight the world on your own.

'You're going to the doctor,' she insisted. 'You're not well.'

Mother was feeling a lot better, but I was now in trouble. I knew that by the expression on the doctor's face when I went to visit him a few days later, after giving in to relentless coaxing from Muriel. He examined me and said, 'Mrs O'Donnell, I think we should get you to the hospital straight away.' The sombre tone of his voice wasn't what I wanted to hear.

Apparently my blood pressure was as high as it could go, and my kidneys were failing. I was rushed by ambulance to hospital in Donegal where I was immediately hooked up to all kinds of contraptions. I was gravely ill, they told my family. Francie was contacted and told about my condition. They informed him that I was going to have to be operated on when all the tests had been carried out, and there was a danger I might not come through it. Needless to say, poor Francie was in a terrible state.

When Francie came home, he went up to the local priest, Father Glacken, and asked him to bless me. Poor Francie was distraught and in tears.

'Francie, I thought you were a stronger man than this,' Father Glacken said to him.

'I don't want to lose her,' Francie sobbed.

Father Glacken opened the drawer of his desk, took out a small portion of salt and gave it to Francie. 'Go up to Julia straight away and give her a taste of this salt,' he ordered him.

Without question, Francie did as he was told. He arrived at the hospital and put a pinch of the salt on my lips. 'Now taste that,' he told me.

'I've been fasting for thirteen days and you're giving me salt,' I said, managing a smile.

'Take it, Julia. It's from Father Glacken,' he said softly. Francie had great faith in the priest.

The following day, Francie arrived before they took me to the table to operate. He asked for the doctor to see how I was.

'Mr O'Donnell, she's doing very well. There'll be no operation,' said the doctor.

Francie was delighted.

'Where this change came from I don't know,

because your wife was in a critical condition last night,' the doctor added.

Francie crossed himself and thought of Father Glacken.

There was still a lot of concern about my condition, however, and the medical staff decided that the best course of action was to induce the birth. They gave me injections, and I suffered for 19 hours in labour before my first son was born. Being two months premature, he was so small I could hold him in the palm of my hand.

We called him John Bosco, and I'll tell you now how he got his name. The night before John was born, there were a lot of visitors to the hospital, and the nuns asked them to pray for me. They said that I had a hard battle ahead of me, and it was a case of trying to save the mother, but there was no hope for the baby.

John Bosco was born on a Saturday, and the following day the same people came to see me. They told me what the nuns had said to them, and how they had gone away, gathered in one house to pray, and made a novena to St John Bosco, praying that both myself and the baby would survive. They then suggested that I should call the newborn John Bosco after the saint who had intervened with the man above to let us come through the ordeal safe and well. To be honest with you, I didn't even know at the time that there was a saint called John Bosco.

Many years later, I read that St John Bosco was an Italian priest who came from a poor background. His father died when he was only two years old, leaving his mother, Margaret Bosco, to support three young boys on her own. Don Bosco went on to become a priest and founded the Salesian Society in 1859, in response to the poverty and desperation he saw among young people in his home town of Turin. He went on to found homes and schools to help them. Today the Salesians are the third-largest order in the Catholic Church, with more than 17,000 priests and brothers and 17,000 sisters in most countries in the world. They are recognized everywhere as leaders in the field of schooling for the poor, looking after the needs of abandoned and neglected children and youths. It was his unselfish dedication and work with the poor youngsters that earned Don Bosco a sainthood: he was beatified by Pope Pius Xl in 1929.

Our firstborn child was duly christened John Bosco, and we resolved that if we were blessed with more wee ones, they would be called Bosco as well. It's a nice name. It saved my life. I thank God, and I thank all who prayed for me that night.

When we took John Bosco home, he was the

tiniest wee thing you ever did see, being a seven-
month baby. You wouldn't find him in a basket or a
cot, so we put him in a shoe box. To this day, if you
ask him, John will delight in telling all and sundry
that he was reared in a shoe box. He was so small
we were told not to bath him as he had just a film of
skin; he didn't even have fingernails. We rubbed
olive oil on him until he was three months old, and
he didn't need a pram until he was six months. Now
John Bosco is a fine man who is married with two
sons – and he's a grandad. So miracles do happen.

Francie and I set up home in Kincasslagh on the
mainland in a house that had been owned by one of
my uncles who had passed on to his eternal reward.
His daughter, being very kind and thoughtful, said to
me, 'Why don't you move into the house and look after
it because we don't want to leave it lying empty.' She
already had a home of her own. We took her up on the
offer, and I would go on to spend the next 20 years
there. My mother, who was from the area, had actually helped with the building of the house. It's a stone
house, and the stone was carried by hand during the
construction. They used to mix the ashes from the
fireplace with lime and sand to cement the stones. It
was a very solid, waterproof house. As good as
anything you'll find in modern times.

Our daughter Margaret was born one year and nine months after John Bosco without any drama. Kathleen was the next one to come along. Francie always came home when one of the children was due to be born.

When I was giving birth to Kathleen, I had Nurse Bridie Doherty with me in the house. Francie was outside with John Bosco, Margaret and relations of mine called Biddy and Neilie McGonagle. They were marching up and down the road outside our home, with Francie playing the flute and the other four drumming on tin cans while they were waiting for the new arrival.

James was born four years after Kathleen. When he was born, the nurse called them in to see the child. John Bosco crept slowly up to the bed and had a peek at his tiny brother. By the look of him, he wasn't too happy with the latest addition to our little clan. He turned to Francie and asked, 'Daddy, are you sure he's ours?' Francie and myself had such a laugh.

And last, but not least, came the boy himself, Daniel, who was born on 12 December 1961. He ended the show – the last of the Boscos. If I have one regret about my married life, it's the fact that I spent most of it being separated from my lovely husband while the children were growing up. Unless you were a fisherman, husbands had no choice but to go away in search of work. It was either that or emigrate to America in search of a new life. We wanted to keep our roots in Ireland and rear the children there, even though we accepted that it would mean me living the life of a single parent while Francie was away.

Like so many other husbands, Francie spent all of our married life working his way around Scotland year in and year out. It was a never-ending cycle of heartbreak, not just for couples but for their children as well. The truly sad thing is that Francie didn't get to see much of his children, and he missed out on the wonderful experience of watching them grow and develop their own little personalities. They loved him dearly, though, and pined for him when he went away. I don't think they ever heard him raise his voice to them, and, despite being a big, strong man, he was gentle and kind. Francie loved those children, and he'd sit them on his knee and tell them stories, or play them a tune on the flute. He was like the Pied Piper when he was in the house. They followed him around wherever he went.

Their excitement would grow and grow in the weeks before Francie was due home on holiday. We'd be lying in bed and Margaret would ask, 'When will Daddy be home?' Then Kathleen would ask the same question. It might be four weeks, and I'd hold up four fingers to them and they'd count: 'One, two, three, four. Will that be long, Mammy?'

'Not too long now,' I'd reply. Every day it would be the same.

'How long more will it be before Daddy is home?' James would ask. And they'd all look at me. As the fingers began to disappear, you could see the excitement mounting and their eyes twinkling with delight.

The night before Francie was due, I'd announce, 'Your daddy will be here in the morning.' And sure they wouldn't sleep a wink with the excitement. Santa Claus never got such a reaction. From sunrise, their little heads would be in the window, patiently waiting for their daddy. When he arrived at the door, they'd be out of the house like greyhounds after a hare. No man ever got a warmer, more loving welcome.

Often he'd only be home for a week in July, and again at Christmas for another week or two. In the spring he'd come home to cut the turf, and we'd all go to the bog with him to help with that job. When we'd arrive at the bog Francie would ask us to go down on our knees and say a decade of the rosary that the weather would stay good until we got the turf home. And when we got the turf home, we had to go down on our knees again and do another decade of the rosary in thanksgiving.

Children being children, the little ones weren't big fans of prayer.

Brief and all as it was, those were happy days when Francie was around the house. Sometimes he'd get a couple of months' work doing fish-processing on the pier in Kincasslagh, just down the road from our house. He'd be able to come home for his dinner in the middle of the day, and that was a real luxury. I lived for that time, but inevitably it would end in sadness and heartbreak when Francie had to leave. I always packed his case when he went away, and it would be full of tears as well as clothes as I cried my eyes out.

It was a terrible life. Before he went away, Francie would ask us all to go down on our knees and then we'd say a decade of the rosary that God would save him and us and that he would come back again. When he returned we'd do the same again to thank God that Daddy was safe and that we were all there to meet him.

Francie, as I said, was a very religious man. He was an exceptionally devout Catholic, and his faith was always a great comfort to him. Father Keegan, a priest we knew in Scotland, tells the story of how Francie braved Arctic weather to attend Sunday Mass when he was away at work in the wintertime, digging ditches and doing drainage. When Father

Keegan woke up one Sunday morning, there was a foot of snow on the ground and the blizzard was still blowing. In the far-off distance he could see a couple of black dots at the end of a field.

Who has cattle out on a day like this? he thought.

A short time later, as he was going into the local church, he realized that the dots were the two familiar figures of Francie and his brother James. They'd walked miles and miles in awful conditions to attend church.

'There was no need for you to come out on a day like this,' Father Keegan told them.

'I wouldn't miss Mass,' Francie replied.

'Father Keegan, on the day I die, and on the day of my funeral, I hope it's snowing,' James remarked. The strange thing about that is, years later when James died and Father Keegan was standing over the grave as the coffin was being lowered into the ground, it was snowing.

Francie also had the cure for what was known at the time as 'the Evil'. This was a lump the size of an egg that came out on the side of a person's face. Francie became a faith-healer when he was given a special prayer by an old man who lived near him. He passed it on to Francie before he died. A seventh son is said to have special healing powers, and even though Francie was an eighth son, there was a set of male twins in his family and that was counted as one.

The special prayer he'd been given went on to perform miracle cures through Francie for many, many people. It was well known that he had this gift, and people would flock to him from near and far with their ailments. No matter how hard his life was at the time, Francie never refused anyone. He had to see the afflicted person over three days. Part of the cure was that he had to attend to the person after midnight and before the sun came up, so he would have to go to them in the middle of the night. And there were times when Francie came home from Scotland to attend to people and he'd stay for the three days. Nothing was too much for Francie. He was very, very good. He would go out in the middle of the night to help anyone. The special prayer was to be known only to Francie himself. He wasn't allowed to tell me or anyone else what it was, and I never did ask him. If he so wished, it was within his gift to pass it on to someone else when the time came.

When he was home, Francie used to enjoy the laughs he got from the children, particularly when they were very young and innocent. As Daniel was the baby in the family, I used to take him with me wherever I went. The only place he never wanted to go with me was to the local church when I'd be going to confession. So, whenever I was visiting someone or somewhere and I didn't want Daniel to come with me, I'd put him off by telling him, 'I'm going to confession, Daniel.' And Daniel would stay behind without a whimper.

At the time we had a dog called Rover, and one day when Daniel was crossing over to a neighbour's house, the dog began to follow him. Daniel was about three at the time, and Francie was out front watching to see that he crossed safely. Daniel turned to Francie and said, 'Daddy, call Rover back. Tell him he can't come because I'm going to confession.'

Francie laughed, and when he told me the story I realized that Daniel saw through my little trick but always played along with it. Even at the age of three he was that smart.

Daniel always slept in my bed as a child when Francie was away working. He could never under-stand why he was evicted every time Daddy came home. 'Can't Daddy sleep somewhere else?' he'd ask. You could see by the expression of thunder on Daniel's little face that he was none too pleased about the change in his regular sleeping arrangement.

The children were great company, especially during the months when Francie was working abroad. The house was always full of life and chatter. I hadn't a minute to myself keeping up with their antics, particularly the boys'. Well, especially young James, who was tall for his age and who spent most his time dreaming up ways to be the centre of attention. I don't know where I got him; he always seemed to be up to some kind of mischief.

Wash day at that time was a major operation. There was no electric washing machine to ease the burden of work. Water was boiled in saucepans on the range and then carried outside to fill up a tub where I would scrub the dirty laundry by hand. It was time-consuming work and tedious too.

One morning I had spent the best part of an hour heating the water and filling a bathtub outside. Then I mixed in the washing soda and slushed it around to create suds. No sooner had I turned my back to fetch the dirty laundry from the house than the bold James was up to his trickery. He just couldn't resist the temptation to tip up the bathtub and empty out all my lovely hot, soapy water. I came around the corner just in time to see him scurrying away from the scene of the crime with a big, cheeky grin on his face.

I grabbed a sally rod and chased after him. Eventually I cornered James and gave him a lash of the sally stick. It didn't seem to bother him in the least. But no matter what mischief he got up to, I couldn't stay mad at James for long. I knew in my heart that there was no real badness in him. He just saw the humour in everything. To him, his antics were just harmless fun, but I didn't always see the funny side of them. And he was forever playing tricks on the rest of the children, silly stuff like hiding their things. That would always cause a row. There was no malice in James, he was just a trickster. But I was forever shouting at him, 'James, if you don't leave them alone I'll give you a lash of the sally rod!' I might as well have been talking to the wall for all the notice that he took of me.

John Bosco was a different young fellow altogether. Although he was older, Bosco was smaller and quiet in himself. You wouldn't know he was around the house if James wasn't taunting him. Then he'd be well able to stand up for himself. Kathleen was a second mother to them all. She was very like myself when I was that age, as she loved helping round the home. As the years went on, her siblings would always turn to Kathleen for advice. She's a great listener, and she'd always be totally honest with them.

Margaret was a great worker too, and she loved to sing. She really had something special for a child so young, and I taught her some lovely old ballads. 'Sing a song for us,' I'd say in the evening. And Margaret would stand in the middle of the floor, close her eyes and sing like she understood all the emotions that were in those songs. But on the occasions when I had to scold Margaret for misbehaving when she was a youngster, she'd get all huffy and march off to her room. Then she'd appear out of it with her little case all packed and announce that she was leaving home. She'd march off down to the strand in Kincasslagh and sit behind a rock. I'd discreetly keep an eye on her from a distance. When she'd eventually realize that no one was coming to get her, you'd see little Margaret slinking back up the road again with the little case. She'd come into the house, ignore everybody and go to her room.

Even without children, our house was always busy. There was an endless stream of visitors coming through the door. No one ever had to knock; they just lifted the latch and walked right in. The kettle would be on, and tea was always on offer. A cup of tea and a chat with the neighbours, there was nothing like it. I was surrounded by lovely people in my neighbourhood, and that compensated in some ways for the loneliness I felt when Francie was away.

As I was an island woman and the only one in the vicinity, people coming over from the local islands would occasionally call too. I was always ready to welcome anyone who was storm-bound. One afternoon a group of fishermen from Tory Island arrived into Kincasslagh pier with a cargo of herring. I took them in for tea as it was a particularly stormy evening. As the time went on, there was no sign of the storm blowing over. In fact, it got considerably worse, posing a real danger to anyone out on the open sea. The men from Tory were very concerned about it, so I told them not to risk the crossing. 'You can stay in our house. I won't have enough beds, but I have a big fire and plenty of food,' I told them.

They took me up on the offer, and it turned out to be a great night. The fishermen had some drink with them to fortify themselves against the elements, and they had a sup of that. Before long a sing song had started. I made plenty of tea and gave them lots of bread that I had baked. The singing continued into the early hours of the morning, and it was an unexpected night of merriment.

My mother, who was staying with us then, was in a bed off the kitchen. The next morning she said, 'That was the finest night of singing I ever heard.'

It broke my heart on those occasions when I'd dwell on how much Francie was missing out in our lives. I longed for the day that he wouldn't have to emigrate to find work. Little did I know that ahead of us lay a terrible tragedy that would tear us apart.

chapter seven

My Darkest Day

IT WASN'T UNTIL 1967 that our family finally moved into the modern age when the local council agreed to provide us with a cottage. For the first time in our lives we were going to have all the mod cons of the times.

Up till then, we were still living with the remnants of a dying era in the house my cousin had kindly loaned to us after her father had died. It still had an old-fashioned open fire, with the cooking being done in pots hanging over the burning coals. There were no electricity and no running water. The house had neither a bathroom nor even a flush toilet – the latter was a tin hut at the end of the garden. The new cottage was going to have all of those modern conveniences. If Donegal County Council had provided us with a castle, the family wouldn't have been more excited.

All we could think of for weeks and weeks as it neared completion was our big move into this bright, spacious, modern cottage. The new dwelling was just across the road from the house we were living in, so we weren't being uprooted from our normal surroundings. It couldn't have been more perfect. The building of the new house provided great entertainment, and some frustration, as we watched it going up, block by block, month after month.

'Mother, they're starting the roof,' Kathleen said one morning.

'Do you think it will be ready next week?' Margaret asked.

'It'll be a wee while yet,' I replied, and their heads hung. The construction work probably seemed like an eternity to the children. And, to be honest, I wasn't very patient myself.

When the shell was completed, we clapped and cheered.

'It won't be long now till we're in our snug new house,' I assured the children. Little did I know that the interior work was a much slower process and that the plumbing, electrical and carpentry jobs would take many more months.

In November, the house was ready for us to occupy. I'd been given a key by one of the workers, but the cottage hadn't been officially handed over to me by the council. The weather had turned bitter, and we were freezing in the old house. I'd look over at the newly built cottage, which seemed so warm and inviting, and I'd wish that we could move in there and then. The weeks went by, the weather got colder and colder, and there was no sign of the notice from Donegal County Council. The postman occasionally called with a letter. I'd be delighted when I'd see one arriving from Francie, but there would be disappointment as well when the council's notice wasn't in the postman's bag.

One day, as I peered out through the frosted window of the old house, I decided that I couldn't wait for the council's red tape to be sorted. We would move over lock, stock and barrel under the cover of darkness that very night. Francie was away working in Scotland, so the family and I hauled over our bits and pieces of furniture, our clothes and whatever other few possessions we had to our name. At 11 p.m. we finally got the beds through the door and set them up in the rooms. Then we tried to settle down to sleep, although that was virtually impossible with the excitement of being in our grand new abode. The wee fella, Daniel, hadn't yet turned six, and I think he was probably more excited than any of us. You'd think to look at him that it was Christmas morning as he raced from room to room examining every nook and cranny. I had a terrible job keeping him away from the taps. He kept turning them on and off to see the water gushing out of them. The flush toilet was going every few minutes, and I don't think nature was working overtime on him. It was just the novelty of it all.

When I wrote to Francie and informed him that we were in the house, he wrote back and told me to make sure that I got the local priest to bless it. 'I hope the council won't be mad at you for going in too soon,' he added. It was another few weeks before the council's official letter arrived, but by that time we had made ourselves at home in our lovely new surroundings. It was a cosy little nest, and I could hardly wait for Francie to come home and see it for himself. For the first time in our married life we finally had a home we could call our own.

I'll never forget the look on Francie's face when he arrived home that Christmas. As the car pulled up, I could see him looking round and admiring the new cottage. We all rushed out to greet him. One of the children took his case, and Francie and I strolled up to the house. As we reached the entrance, he put a hand on each side of the door frame and said, 'It's nice to be going into your own home.' That was one of Francie's happiest days: to see us all enjoying such comfort in a lovely, modern dwelling.

I had been saving for about a year to buy new things for the house. When you go into a new home you have everything to buy for it. I made extra money by knitting sweaters and selling them. I also tried to save something out of the money Francie sent home to provide for our living expenses. Then I'd go out and search for bargains. Not a penny was squandered as I gradually accumulated the essential items and some decorations that we needed for the new place. Shiny new pots and pans sat on top of the range. There was a dresser in the kitchen, all decked out with lovely cups, saucers and plates. I'd bought colourful lampshades for the electric lights, and there were new curtains for the windows. I got down on my hands and knees with a bucket of soapy water and a scrubbing brush and I washed every inch of the floor to get rid of the dust. I chipped away at the solid lumps of plaster that were splattered here and there. Later I bought cheap lino for the floor covering. It looked real nice.

'You've done a great job, Julia,' Francie said after settling in. 'I'm so happy here in our own home.'

That happy period was short-lived. After a few months it was getting close to the time for Francie to leave again to pick up work in Scotland. He was nearly 49 years old, and the hard life he'd endured was beginning to take its toll on his health. Not that he ever complained. You'd never hear Francie moan about his lot. He just got on with it.

'Daddy, don't go away this year,' Margaret pleaded with him.

I could see Francie's eyes watering. It was emotionally draining for him to have to leave his loved ones, particularly when he was growing weary of his terrible lifestyle. I knew it was a torture for him to have to leave.

'You don't need to be going to Scotland. Stay here with us, we'll be grand from now on,' Margaret begged. She loved her daddy. They all did.

'I'll go this year, but I won't go any more,' Francie finally relented.

There were still a few weeks to go before he left, but I could see that Francie wasn't himself. He shuffled where he used to strut along. And he had difficulty catching his breath.

One morning when I woke up, he was sitting up in the bed. I yawned and propped myself up on the pillow. 'How are you feeling today, Francie?' I asked.

'I'm fine,' he replied. Then he smiled. 'Do you know, you're some sleeper,' he added. 'I have said a rosary for myself and one for you, one for John Bosco, one for Margaret, one for James, one for Kathleen and one for Daniel. I've said one for everyone who is sick and one for the dead.' Francie shuffled a pile of novenas with his hands. 'Do you see that pile of wee leaflets? I've read through all of those while you were sleeping.'

I smiled at him. 'The people who get the benefit of them will be eternally grateful to you.'

I got up out of bed, and later, as I sat writing letters, I heard him on the move. When I went to see if he wanted some breakfast, I got a terrible fright. Francie was struggling to catch his breath.

'I'm not too good, Julia,' he sighed, the blood draining from his face.

'We'll get the doctor down, Francie,' I said.

He nodded in agreement. I knew then that he must be feeling real bad because Francie wouldn't want the doctor unless he was in serious pain.

By the time the doctor arrived, Francie's complexion had turned a deathly grey. The doctor took one look at him and said, 'We'll get you up to the hospital straight away for an X-ray, Francie. I'll call for an ambulance.'

We had no phone in the house, so the doctor drove down to the public phone in the village to make the call. After a short time he returned to the house with the news that there was no ambulance to be got. 'I'll take Francie to the hospital myself,' he said. As he walked him to the car, Francie was struggling more and more to catch his breath.

I was standing outside the front door in a pair of

slippers watching him, and my heart was pounding against my chest with fright. 'Wait till I get my shoes and I'll go with you,' I said. I rushed inside, but I was in such a state of panic and shock that I couldn't find my shoes.

'I'll have to go,' the doctor shouted before slamming the door of the car.

I went back outside and the car was heading off round the turn on the road. I could see Francie still struggling for breath as he looked back to see if I was coming.

The time passed like an eternity as I waited for news of Francie's condition. What was the X-ray going to show? As I stood at the gate waiting for a cousin of mine to return with information, a neighbour stopped to enquire about Francie. I was telling him that I was just waiting on news of the X-ray when a car pulled up beside us. There was a priest in the back, but there was nothing unusual about a car stopping as drivers were always calling looking for directions.

The priest got out of the car and then I saw that he was being followed by Biddy, one of our relatives. My first thought was that Biddy had heard in the village that Francie had been taken away and that she was coming looking for news of him.

It was the priest who stopped and spoke. 'Are you Julia?' he asked.

'I am,' I said, and a terrible feeling came over me.

The priest looked down at his shoes. I knew then that he had come to me with some awful news.

'Father, is there anything wrong?' I heard myself asking.

'Yes,' he said, his head shaking.

My heart was racing. 'Have you good news or bad news?' I heard myself asking.

'I have good news and bad news,' the priest replied, lifting his head.

'Is Francie dead?' I asked, fearing that I already knew the answer.

'I'm afraid he is after dying,' the priest said quietly.

When I look back on it, I think that I went into shock at that moment because I didn't immediately react to this dreadful news that the priest was telling me. That my Francie was gone.

Then the priest started to speak again. 'The good news is that your Francie got the last rites before he died, by a strange coincidence,' he revealed. 'All the other priests are away on a retreat. I say Mass in Dungloe hospital once a year, but I wasn't due to say it today. I met Biddy yesterday, and she asked me where I was going to be saying Mass today. I told her I was going to say it in Kincasslagh. Biddy then said how she was hoping it was Dungloe, as she was looking for a lift there. I decided then that I'd go and say the Mass in the hospital, and that's how I was up there to give Francie the last rites.'

Francie had once told a cousin of mine that he prayed he would never die without a priest. So he was granted that request.

The priest told me more of the details, how Francie had died just as he was entering the hospital. It was God that had saved me from going with him because I wouldn't have wanted to be there when he passed away.

I was still in shock. I heard myself asking, 'Father, did he have time to make his confession?'

'My good woman,' he answered, 'that man had no need to make a confession. He went straight to heaven.'

The priest shook my hand as I turned to enter the house. It broke my heart to see the commotion inside. The children had overheard the whole conversation and knew that their daddy was dead. They were inconsolable, and I just wanted to curl up and die myself. They looked like a pitiful bunch of lost souls as they tried to take it all in. They were heartbroken that life could be so cruel to them: they curled up in corners crying. I looked at wee Daniel, only six years old, and thought how unfair it was that he would never really remember his daddy because he was so young.

Later the body of my darling Francie came home in a coffin. As four men struggled to manoeuvre it through the front door, I sobbed at the thought that it would be Francie's last time coming into his own house. He'd had so little time to enjoy it. As they opened the lid of the box I felt my legs go weak, and I burst into loud fits of sobbing. A neighbour put her arm around me to calm me. I stroked Francie's forehead and kissed it. He looked like he was just asleep. We laid him out in a candlelit room, which had a large crucifix on the wall. The wake went by in a blur for me. Neighbours came and went over a couple of days, paying their respects and offering support. 'Sorry for your trouble, Julia, if there's anything we can do, you know where we are,' they'd say. I was grateful to have everyone around to comfort me, but no one could bring my Francie back to his family.

No words can describe the pain in our house on the day of the funeral. The wailing of the children would have melted the hardest of hearts. Poor little Daniel didn't really know what was going on, but he became very upset when he saw the coffin leaving the house. Daniel clung to it and cried, 'Don't youse take me daddy away. Bury him in the garden.'

He held my hand and pleaded, 'Please, Mammy, don't let them take our dad away. We need him here at home.' He kept crying, 'Everyone will have a daddy now but us.' Then he asked, 'Will Dad ever come back?'

I could barely get the words out and my heart was breaking as I said, 'No, Daniel, God wanted him and we have to let him go.'

I travelled in the hearse with the coffin, my hand resting on the head of it until we reached the chapel. When they lifted the coffin out of the hearse down at the church and placed it on a trolley, I helped to push it up the aisle and sat beside it during the funeral Mass. Afterwards I followed the coffin to the lonely graveyard and kissed the head of the box before it was lowered into the cold, dark earth. Every sickening thud of the clay hitting the wood felt like a nail being driven through my heart. It was a horrible sound and such a cold, cold feeling. I left the graveyard that day with a black cloud hanging over me, and I doubted that I would ever see a sunny day again.

I looked at the children, the poor souls, and wondered what was going to become of us all without Francie. It was going to be a heavy cross for us all to bear.

There was no consoling the children in the days that followed. I tried to tell them that Daddy was still with us and looking after us; it was just that he wasn't physically there, and we couldn't see or touch him. I would look at the five of them and say, 'There's a part of your daddy in every one of you.'

Daniel didn't want to go back to school. 'I can't go, Mammy,' he'd say. 'You will be lonely without Dad.'

It was a long, hard, painful road trying to overcome our grief. There were moments when it became too unbearable. Kathleen stood with her back to the wall one night at bedtime roaring, 'I want Daddy.'

My heart went out to her, but what could I do? 'Kathleen, we all want Daddy,' I said, trying to calm her. 'Daddy is away to heaven. He's in a lovely place. Try to be happy for him.' But I was engulfed with loneliness myself. At that moment I could never foresee any joy in my life, ever again. Even though Francie had spent every year of our married life working abroad, I had the comfort of knowing that he was always there in times of trouble. He was just a boat and train trip away from me. I knew that if there was a problem with one of the children, no matter how big or small, I had Francie to consult and share the responsibility.

On the few occasions in my adult life when I'd seen a young man dying and leaving a family behind him, I'd said to Francie, 'If that ever happened to you, I wouldn't want to live another day. I would want to go into another coffin and go out after you into the grave. I couldn't bear to see anything happen to you.' But when it happens, of course, you get the strength from somewhere to deal with it. I didn't have time to feel sorry for myself and my own loss because I was distracted by the children and their mourning for their daddy. I was also sick with the worry of how we were going to get by without him. Francie had always been the main breadwinner. Now I was on my own with a family of five. I cried myself to sleep worrying about our future. What was going to become of us? There was very little money in the family's coffers because we had spent a lot on new things for the house, little knowing what terrible fate lay in waiting around the corner for us. Then I had the funeral expenses and the cost of a headstone for the grave. When everything was paid, I was virtually penniless. What was I going to do? I prayed to God and to Francie to help me.

The widow's pension from the government wasn't a lot, but at least it would cushion the blow. To qualify for the pension I had to produce a death certificate, so I sent Margaret away on the bus to get it from a doctor. Some time later Margaret arrived home in floods of tears. The doctor had told her it would be four months before we'd get the certificate. Margaret said she had pleaded with the doctor to give it to her there and then as the family was in a desperate state with no money. He had glared at her over the wee, round glasses sitting on the tip of his nose and said sharply, 'You'll have to wait like all the rest. Your father was no more important than anyone else.'

Margaret was horrified by those words. 'My daddy was very important,' she shouted in a fit of rage and hurt as she stormed out of the doctor's.

By the time she reached home, the poor girl was in a terrible state and dreading having to break the bad news to me. I was very angry when I heard about the attitude of the doctor and the way he spoke to Margaret, so I went down to the local priest, Father MacAteer, and told him what had happened. I asked for his advice as to what I should do. I told him about the desperate financial state that we were in.

'Don't you worry, Mrs O'Donnell. We'll get it all sorted out for you,' Father MacAteer said as he tried to calm me down.

He gave me a letter stating that Francie and myself had been married in Kincasslagh and that he had been the priest who had buried Francie. This was sufficient for me to be granted the pension, and it came through a few weeks later.

I sat down one night and tried to work out the sums, hoping that we could make ends meet. The widow's pension didn't stretch very far. Without more money coming into the house, we were going to be in dire straits. Day in and day out I prayed that something would turn up to change our fortunes. Then one day a letter arrived from America with some welcome news. It was from a man called Matt Cavanagh, who was married to one of my cousins. Matt had heard that life had become a struggle for us. I knew him by reputation to be a very kind and caring man. Our tale of woe had reached him through family members; they say that bad news travels fast and to far-off corners. It had troubled Matt's mind to think of a family in need back home in Ireland, especially after enduring the pain of losing a loved one.

Matt had a proposition for me. He said that if I was willing to hand-knit sweaters, he would find a market for them in America. As I read the words over and over, the dark cloud lifted. Knitting, of course, was second nature to me, and to be able to earn a living from it for my family was a great opportunity. It had been such a long time since I'd smiled, but Matt's good-natured gesture lit up my face with joy when I read his words. I wrote back to him that very same day accepting his kind offer.

In a strange way the struggle to provide for my family and my concentration on that effort helped me to cope with my grief over Francie's sudden passing. It kept me busy, and my mind was constantly occupied by the work and the effort to produce as many sweaters as was humanly possible for me to knit every day. Once I started my new little industry, there was no stopping me. All day, every day, you'd find me in a corner with two needles dancing between my fingers. In periods when I needed extra cash, I'd stay up knitting through the night when every other body was sleeping. I'd finish off a new batch of sweaters and then make up packages for the mail the next day. Sometimes it would be 4 a.m. when I'd finally fall into my bed from exhaustion. I didn't care about the tiredness. The work meant that I was self-sufficient, and as long as the market for the sweaters lasted I knew that we would be okay. We were going to get through this terrible time. Matt has since passed on, and I'm sure he's in heaven with Francie. God rest his soul.

Although I was now earning money, I had to account for every penny to make sure that there was always something in the kitty to pay the bills. I had to be thrifty, and I had no spare cash to pay people for jobs like turf-cutting. When I needed to stock up on winter fuel I would get local children to help me in the bog, which was 6 miles away from the house. The turf had to be cut and dried and then carried home. Then it was stacked up outside the house and covered to protect it from the rain. And that pile of turf kept us in fuel for the whole of the winter.

When the cheque arrived from Matt in America, I'd cash it in the local shop and then stash the money under my mattress. There was always some money stored to pay a bill. One day I lifted the mattress to get some cash and to my horror there was nothing underneath it. I was always very careful with the money, and I felt sure that I had some savings. Matt's cheque was due any day, but I needed cash at that moment to stock up on food. I knelt down and prayed to St Anthony, the patron saint of lost things and missing persons. Then I lifted up the mattress again, and this time there was a ten-shilling note tucked away at the head of the bed. Now, whether that was there the first time and I just didn't spot it, I cannot say. Maybe I didn't raise the mattress high enough. I prefer to think that it was St Anthony performing his little miracle for me. From then on I never looked back. I always made ends meet.

Today I always remember Matt in my prayers, and I will be eternally grateful for his kindness. Four members of his family travelled over to Ireland on holidays in 2005 for the first time. They were staying just across the road from me, and we got to spend some time together. I spoke with them about Matt and told them of the difference he had made to my life and that of my family shortly after I lost Francie. I had a letter that Matt had written to me around that time, and I gave it to them as a keepsake. They were glad to get their father's letter, and really loved their time in Donegal, a place that had been so close to their father's heart.

There was never any question that I would look for another man to love and support me in life after Francie died. I never for one moment considered getting married again. I would never put another man's ring on my finger. I thought the world of Francie and he thought the world of me. And I would never have another man enter the lives of my children. NEVER.

Granny McGonagle (my mother) with Margaret and Daniel.

One of my favourite photographs of Margaret as a young woman.

Margo & The Keynotes

Margaret became a house-
hold name in Ireland with
The Keynotes.

She was only a wee child
when she joined the band.

God blessed my Daniel with the gift of a lovely singing voice. Now he has fans
all over the world.

Daniel singing with his friend Cliff Richard on stage at The Point,
Dublin, in 2006.

Through Daniel's career, I have met many celebrities. Here we are with Liz Dawn, better known as *Coronation Street*'s Vera Duckworth.

Margaret with American country legend, Dolly Parton. They recorded a song together called 'God's Colouring Book' in 1997.

I never expected to meet Royalty, but here I am in the company of Prince Charles on the day Daniel (pictured with Majella) received an MBE. He even kissed my hand!

My son James (front) and myself, with the Sam Maguire cup, won by Donegal in the 1992 All Ireland Football Final.

I am so happy to have lived to enjoy moments like this with
great-granddaughter, Sarah.

My very special
cousin Willie
McDevitt, pictured
here next to my
daughter-in-law
Eileen.

My oldest grandchild Frankie, with his daughter Sarah.

My beloved grandson Joey, with great-grandchild Sarah.

Today I'm in my twilight years and happy that I'm not
hidden away and forgotten.

chapter eight

Margaret

GOD NEVER BLESSED me with a singing voice, but I've always loved music. Growing up I memorized the words to all the old ballads I heard from our elders on Owey. It's just that I could never sing them.

As a youngster I'd listen almost in a trance when some of the old men – and one or two of the grandmothers – on the island would sing in the corner of someone's house at night, surrounded by neighbours. Those wonderful ballads had been passed down from generation to generation. Even though I couldn't chirp like a bird myself, I always appreciated a good singer when I heard one.

I knew from the moment my cute little daughter Margaret began singing that she possessed something special. Today, they call it the 'X Factor', although nobody has been able to describe what that is. Whatever it may be, I was convinced that Margaret had it, and I encouraged her to sing at every opportunity, whether in the house or at concerts down in the local parish hall. I had retained a fine store of ballads in my head from long ago, and I taught Margaret the words to all of them. She was quick to learn and I could see that she had a real passion for it.

'Give us a song there, Margaret,' local people would say when she called to their house on a visit. Annie McGarvey, the blacksmith's daughter, lived across the road and she had struck up a very close bond with Margaret. She loved to hear the wee girl sing. It was the same in every house Margaret called to. 'Ah, you'll give us an auld song,' they'd say.

At that time there was a very popular local band called the Keynotes. The band members were Enda Breslin, Johnny Gallagher, Condy Boyle, Tony Boyle, Eddie Quinn, Charlie McCole, Paddy Joe O'Donnell and Hughie Ward. They were a nice, clean-cut band, dressed in sharp suits and they had become a household name in Donegal.

The Keynotes were also aware of Margaret's talent as a singer. There was no dancing during Lent in those days, so the band used to get involved in a little drama group, staging shows in the local hall for charity. During the interval the local priest, Father Deegan, would get Margaret up to sing. So the Keynotes recognized then that she was very talented.

In September 1964 two members of the Keynotes, Tony Boyle and Condy Boyle, came to me and asked if I would allow Margaret to join the band as their lead singer, Enda Breslin, was leaving to join the Garda.

'I'll have to talk to her father, but I don't see why not,' I agreed.

I thought maybe she could sing an odd night with them for a small fee. The money would certainly be welcome and it would be no great ordeal for Margaret. I'm sure that she didn't have an ambition to be in show business at the time, as she was far too young and innocent to be thinking about what road she was going to go down in life. It was more a case that she really enjoyed singing and the applause of the crowd.

I began to think that if Margaret could become a singer in a band when she left school it would give her a job at a time when work was hard to come by. It would mean that she wouldn't have to emigrate to make a life for herself, and I wouldn't lose her.

I wrote to Francie and told him that the Keynotes wanted her to become a regular singer with the band. Being a great singer and a musician himself, he was delighted to hear the news. His response was that as long as I was sure that no harm would come to Margaret then he was happy to let her go with the band. It would be good for her, he felt. His other concern was for her education. He didn't want it to affect her schooling. She could sing at weekends and during her school holidays. Margaret danced a jig around the kitchen when she heard the news. She was so happy when she got Francie's blessing.

When I took Margaret to perform with them in a place called Ardara, the reaction she got was incredible. The hall was heaving with young couples out for a night of dancing. But when Margaret began singing the whole atmosphere suddenly changed. Instead of dancing, the crowd stopped in their tracks and stood enthralled as they listened to the rich tones coming from this slip of a schoolgirl. When she finished the first number, the crowd went wild; they were clapping, cheering, whistling and calling, 'More! More!'

Little Margaret just couldn't stop smiling as she stood among the band that night and soaked up the adulation. I think it was at that moment that her fate was sealed. She was destined to become an entertainer. Margaret went on to sing three more songs before she left the stage. And not for one second did she show any nerves. It looked like she was born to be there. Afterwards, I chatted with the Keynotes and the boys were all talking about the reaction of the crowd that night. They had never experienced anything like it. I think they realized that they were on to something big.

The twists and turns of life are strange. I never dreamt that in my 40s I'd be on the road with a show band. But that's exactly where I ended up as I accompanied Margaret and the Keynotes to dances at venues around Donegal. I would travel with someone from the band and sit in the dance hall for the whole night when they were playing. I was watching Margaret grow into a professional singer. Now, however, she was no longer known as Margaret to the public. My little girl, the popular singer, had become known to fans of the Keynotes as Margo. This was the stage name she had taken with the band. Within a few months the Keynotes had become the biggest attraction in Donegal and the surrounding counties. Everyone was talking about this amazing wee girl who was singing with them. The Keynotes had even altered their stage style to complement their little lead singer. They were now wearing specially designed matching cardigans – just like Margaret's.

Little did I realize as I travelled with her during her early days as a singing schoolgirl, the truly incredible impact that my daughter would have throughout Ireland and among the Irish in Britain.

Any money Margaret made at that time she handed over to me, and I kept an account of it. My intention was to give it all back to her some day. But things didn't work out that way.

Shortly before his final trip home from Scotland, Francie sent Margaret the lyrics to a great song called 'Bonny Irish Boy'. He told her in a letter to learn the words and that when he arrived home he would give her the air of it. Coming from her daddy, this song was extra special. Margaret learned it and Francie gave her the tune to it upon his return. When she later sang it for the Keynotes, they recognized that it had real potential to become a hit. Everyone loved it so much they decided that 'Bonny Irish Boy' and another song called 'Dear God' would be their first record to go on release. Margaret nearly jumped through the roof of our kitchen when she heard the news.

The day that 'Bonny Irish Boy' was due to be played on Irish radio for the first time should have been a moment of great joy and celebration. Instead, our whole family had been plunged into a big, dark pit of sorrow. That was the same day Margaret's darling daddy suddenly died. It was such an incredibly cruel coincidence. When tragedy struck, 'Bonny Irish Boy' was immediately withdrawn from the Radio Eireann show as a mark of respect.

I'll never forget Margaret's reaction when it was played on the programme just three weeks later. We listened to the news and then 'Bonny Irish Boy' came on. Margaret had been sitting stiffly on a bench in front of the fire. The moment she heard the music starting, she leapt up, jumped over the seat and made a dash to her bedroom in floods of tears. She was inconsolable. 'That was Daddy's song and he never got to hear the record. If only I'd known that he was going to die I would have got a tape and played it to him,' she sobbed.

Later, we took a recording of the song over to Francie's grave and we played it. As the sound of 'Bonny Irish Boy' reverberated around the grave-yard, our heartache spilled out.

The success of the song was bittersweet. It went on to become a Top 20 hit.

Although he was no longer physically with us, I know that Francie had an influence on the fortunes of his family from beyond the grave. Just a couple of years after he died, Margaret had blossomed into one of Ireland's biggest female singers. Everywhere she performed there were crowds queuing to see her. She was a superstar in Ireland at that time. There really was no one else like her. The excitement Margaret created wherever she went was something you'd normally associate with Hollywood stars. 'Mother, I can't believe what I'm seeing. All those people coming to see me. It's just incredible,' she would tell me.

Margaret had blossomed into a very attractive young woman. On stage she was larger than life, even though she was just 5 feet 4 inches tall. She looked like a young Cilla Black. By then her stage image had changed. She was wearing the fashion of the time – a mini skirt! And along with the joy of seeing Margaret become a success as a singer was the fear that she was moving away from me.

By the early 1970s, Margaret had formed her own band, Country Folk. We had grown accustomed to hearing her records on the radio. But when she released a song called 'I'll Forgive and I'll Try to Forget', it was the first time that she had a number-one hit. She was just 17 years old and there was great excitement, not just in the O'Donnell home but all over Donegal. Everyone was so thrilled and proud that one of their own had got to the top of the charts. With the celebrations that followed you'd think that the county had won the Sam Maguire, the coveted trophy that goes to the All Ireland football champions every year.

Margaret shared her good fortune with the family and was a great source of financial support to me from the moment she started performing with bands.

I was still knitting the sweaters and watching the pennies, but the dire circumstances in which I'd found myself after Francie's sudden death had now eased. However, I had lost my influence over Margaret and that was now my biggest concern. That is the natural course of life as children grow into young adults, but Margaret was in a business where there were so many temptations and I felt the need to question her frequently about her lifestyle even though I had no reason to suspect that she was doing anything wrong.

Margaret and myself are very alike in the sense that we both have strong personalities. She had become very independent in her early teenage years and wanted to live her life as she deemed fit. She was no longer willing to accept me as a figure of authority. Even though I had hoped that by finding work as a singer Margaret wouldn't be forced to emigrate, she did leave me. And, as she was old enough and able to support herself with a good wage, there was very little I could do about it. Margaret moved away, first to Dublin and then to Galway. I was very upset over this conflict in our lives, and I fretted over her when she was away from home.

Margaret will tell you herself that she rebelled against me. She had always been a lot closer to her father. She was Daddy's girl. If there was something she needed to talk about, she would go to Francie to discuss it. And when Francie died, she remained Daddy's girl. She still didn't feel that she could confide in me. It's not that Margaret and I didn't have love for each other, but she had a mind of her own and she wasn't shy about telling you what was on it. She paid no heed to any advice I had to offer. It was something I had to accept. But of course it didn't stop me offering advice where I saw the need. It would have broken my heart if anything bad had happened to her.

Despite our disagreements, I was proud of Margaret, proud of her achievements and delighted to see so many people in Ireland falling under her spell as a singer. Everywhere I went, people would introduce me as 'Margo's mother'. One of the early highlights of Margaret's career was the night she appeared on the *Late Late Show*, which was hosted by Gay Byrne, one of Ireland's greatest and best-loved broadcasters. It was the most popular TV chat show in Ireland. If you got the chance to appear on the *Late Late Show* then you had truly made it. Everyone in Ireland would see you because everything stopped on a Saturday night when the *Late Late Show* was on the telly.

There was incredible excitement in the family and in the entire county of Donegal when the news came through that Margo was going to sing on the show.

Around that time, Hughie Green was a big star on British TV as the host of a talent contest called *Opportunity Knocks*. My own mother loved that show and watched it religiously. She thought Hughie Green was the bee's knees. Whenever he gave a wave on the telly, she truly believed that he was waving at her, and she would wave back at him. The whole family thought this was hilarious, God bless her innocence. And no one had the heart to tell her the truth.

When my mother heard that Margaret was going to be on the *Late Late Show*, she said, 'Be sure to give me a wave, Margaret.'

'I will, and wear your best clothes when you're watching,' Margaret told her.

I didn't go to the *Late Late Show* with Margaret as I was looking after my mother. But I sat in front of the television filled with joy and pride as my daughter was introduced by Gay Byrne before singing one of her big hits. Her granny, dressed in her Sunday best, didn't take her eyes off the small screen. As the studio audience burst into wild applause at the end, Margaret gave a little wave. Her granny smiled and waved back.

Margaret was given a hero's welcome upon her return to Donegal. The entire county turned out to greet her. If she had won the Eurovision Song Contest there wouldn't have been as big a reaction as there was to that first appearance on the *Late Late Show*. Before she finally made it home, we told Margaret what my mother had been wearing as she watched the show. When Margaret walked in, her granny was delighted to see her. I could see her face light up with a mixture of admiration and joy.

'That was a lovely outfit you had on,' Margaret said, and she went on to describe it.

Granny gave a little smile. 'Well, good God, I knew that Hughie Green could see me,' she announced.

Margaret glanced over at me but kept a straight face.

We both laughed inside. Poor Mother.

I remember the first time I saw a television, I had been married for many years. John Phil, a neighbour across the road, got one in his house. And it became a great source of interest among my own children, particularly John Bosco and Margaret, who used to sit on a grassy hill and look in John Phil's window at it. In due course, we rented one ourselves. In those early days there was nothing on the television during the day. You'd turn it on and all you'd see was a test card. It wouldn't come on till the news at 6 p.m. My mother, when she was with us, would always watch the news. She'd tidy up her hair and sit in a chair in front of the television. A man called Charles Mitchell was the newsreader and he'd come on and say, 'Good evening.' And my mother would say, 'Hello!' It was so real to her.

A lot of older people at the time couldn't figure out television at all. We had a neighbour called Joe Doalty and one night while he was visiting us there was an ad on the television for floor-cleaning liquid. A woman known as 'Supergran' was showing a girl how to use it. The ad came on three times while Joe was in the house. Shaking his head, Joe remarked, 'Isn't that a stupid young wan there. Three times that woman is after showing her how to use that floor cleaner and she still doesn't know how to do it!' Margaret was doubled over laughing in the corner. It was the funniest thing ever.

It was the same with the telephone when it eventually arrived in Kincasslagh. It was a turn-handle phone and it was operated through the local post office. After 10 p.m. you had to go on to what they called a 'party line'. Several people shared the same line and each house that had a phone knew by the number of rings whether it was for them. If it was five rings it was for us. A neighbour called Pat Neil Pat, who was on our line, had three rings. One night the phone rang five times, but when I answered it I could hear Pat Neil Pat on the line and the operator talking to him.

'How many rings did you hear, sir?' the operator was asking.

'I heard five, but it should only be three,' Pat replied. He'd been expecting a call.

We laughed, thinking of Pat sitting by the phone and getting all hot and bothered when it rang five times.

As time went on, Margaret became more and more popular. She went on to popularize a new form of music generally referred to as 'country and Irish'. Indeed, she would become affectionately known as 'Margo, the Queen of Country and Irish' by her fans and the music critics.

Everything was now going so well for Margaret that my concern for her welfare had eased. It was time to let go of my child. She was now a young adult making her own way in the world. As hard as it is to do, especially with a daughter, you have to cut the strings and let them off sometime. Margaret herself had long since made the break, but now I had to do that in my own mind. Of course, you never stop worrying about your children, even when they do become adults. And sometimes those concerns come to haunt you, as I would discover.

One day in the early 1970s, as I was busy making pancakes in the kitchen, John Bosco arrived. I knew immediately by his expression that something was troubling him.

'What's up with you, Bosco?' I asked.

'There's been an accident,' he said.

My heart nearly jumped out of my chest. 'What's happened?' I asked in a state of panic.

'It's Margaret. She's been in a crash,' Bosco said quietly.

'She's not dead?' I asked, gripped by fear.

'No, no, but she's in hospital,' he said.

'Hospital? Oh, Bosco, Bosco. What's wrong with her?' I cried, realizing that it was serious.

'I don't know. But she's not going to die, I know that much. She's going to be all right. As soon as you're ready we'll go to Galway,' Bosco said, trying to calm me.

Margaret had been driving to perform at a carnival in Corofin, between Tuam and Galway city, when the crash happened. A car drove out from a pub and went straight into her path. It happened in a flash, giving Margaret no chance to avoid a collision.

It was the kind of news that every parent dreads. We got to Galway as soon as we could. Margaret was in intensive care. It was serious. She had a lot of injuries. They included head injuries, which gave us the most concern. My heart was pounding against my chest when I saw the reality of the situation. Would she be able to walk and talk and do all the things she loved, including singing, ever again? We were reassured by the medical people that, although Margaret had a long, hard road ahead of her, she would make a full recovery.

It was a terrible time in her life. Although she was eventually released from hospital, she had to return as an outpatient every week for a full year. I'm sure it felt like an eternity to her. It must have seemed like there was no light at the end of the tunnel. She became very depressed. Her life at that moment seemed so bleak. There seemed to be no end to her suffering.

After her accident Margaret suffered a series of blackouts. She was put on a course of medication to counteract them. She was on the medication for six years.

She went back touring with the band after she recovered, but Margaret tells me today that she has no memory of being on stage, or of any of the happenings in her life, during that period. 'I don't remember six years. They are wiped out,' she confessed to me.

As she wasn't living at home when she returned to the stage, I had no idea for some time that Margaret's life had taken a turn for the worse. I was delighted that she was able to return to performing. She was still one of the biggest singing stars touring Ireland. But, despite the fact that she had become a much loved singer all over Ireland, Margaret now felt insecure going on stage in front of a crowd, and she fretted over how a new album would be received by the public and the critics. In moments like that she would get into a terrible black state.

Margaret loved singing, but she despised the business side of her career. By all accounts it wasn't a very nice industry. I know from Margaret that some people in the music industry used and abused her. They took advantage of her, particularly when she was vulnerable during times when she was struggling to cope with life. As one of Ireland's top female stars, she should have been a millionaire. But she never got what she was entitled to.

Margaret managed to keep her singing career going because she wasn't feeling down all of the time. A year would go by without any great trauma, but then something would happen and she'd fall back into a deep, dark place. As a mother it was terrible for me to see her going through this torture. It was nearly as hard on me to see Margaret going through such turmoil in her life as it had been losing Francie. There wasn't a night would go by without me praying for her, praying that the light would come back into her life. And there were times when I cried myself to sleep with the worry, fearing that something terrible would happen to her.

Her own determination along with counselling helped Margaret to eventually find peace in her life. Thank God she came through it in the end.

Despite the clash of personalities and the many rows we had, Margaret and I became very close as the years went by. I think that because she spoke her mind during our arguments and because I defended and explained my position, we got to know each other better than if we had not been involved in that kind of communication. It was definitely a learning process for both of us.

Today I have the most wonderful communication with Margaret. No matter what I have concerns about, I will pick up the phone and talk it over with her. That's not to say I don't have the same relationship with my daughter Kathleen, who has been so close to me through all the years. I do. But I'm so glad that I have that respect and friendship with Margaret after all we've been through.

I didn't realize we had become so united until Margaret turned to me one day and said: 'You know, Mother, I haven't got a closer friend today than you.'

I burst into tears.

chapter nine

Daniel

L OOKING AT DANIEL standing by the grave of his daddy in the lonely country graveyard, my heart was torn to pieces at the thought of him growing up never really knowing Francie. He was too young to lose such a wonderful man from his life. Too young to appreciate all his daddy's fine qualities. Too young to learn from him. So many years had already been stolen from Daniel and his daddy through emigration. They'd had such a short time together. Really it was only snatched moments that Francie enjoyed with all of the children. And then, just as he was making plans to retire from those long and lonely trips in search of employment, God called him. Sometimes it is hard to accept the hand of God, but it is a part of our journey through life. There will always be trials and tribulations.

At just six years of age, Daniel had no idea of this great loss. He knew, of course, that Francie had gone to God. But then, as far as Daniel was concerned, his daddy was always coming and going. This time, naturally, he would not be coming back. But at such a tender age, Daniel didn't really understand all of this. I yearned for his innocence so that my own pain would go away, and I know he sensed my terrible heartache. I never let him out of my sight after his father died. I was always worried that I would lose him too. Even though I love all of my children equally, I have to admit that Daniel was always a bit special.

Daniel was a very comical child too. I remember how on his first day setting off on foot to school, with his teddy bear under his arm, he stopped to chat to some council workers who were digging a water drain down the road by our house. He told them that he was starting school and said that he wasn't sure whether he was going to like it or not. The journey to the schoolhouse was 2 miles, and I went up to meet him on the way home. Spotting Daniel as we walked hand in hand down the road, the council workers called him over. 'Well, Daniel, did you have a good day at school?' one asked.

'I did,' said Daniel.

'And what's the teacher like?' the man enquired.

'Oh, she's lovely,' said Daniel. 'She has a miniskirt on her.'

The council workers leaned on their shovels and roared with laughter.

I have only one memory of being really angry with Daniel when he was a child. And that's because I was distraught with fear that he had been drowned in an accident. He went off to play without telling me that he was leaving and where he was going, and when the tide came in below our house Daniel was nowhere to be seen. I went out searching for him around the area, shouting his name. There was no reply. He had disappeared. I grew more frantic as the time went on. Had the sea taken my Daniel?

There's a tower near our house, and that's where I eventually found him. He had gone up exploring inside the tower. I was in a terrible state by the time I eventually got him. I gave him a right good telling-off for being away like that without letting me know. It was one of the few times that there was a cross word between us.

The year after Francie's death was a special time in the life of young Daniel. That was the year he made his First Communion, which is one of the big events in the Catholic church. It should have been a day of great joy and celebration; instead, there was a dark cloud over the family as their daddy was missing from the gathering. Francie had always made the effort to get home for occasions like that. I put on a brave face that day so as not to spoil it for

Daniel, who was so excited about receiving this sacrament, but I was heartbroken.

Daniel looked very smart as he joined the other young people in the church when they went to receive Holy Communion. The suit he was wearing, with short pants, looked good as new on him. Yet it had been serving the boys in the family for many years; John Bosco had first worn it 13 years earlier when he'd made his First Communion. Then it was worn by James on his big day. The jacket was a wee bit long, but it did the job. Nowadays people book restaurants and hold lavish family parties on the day of a First Communion. Daniel's treat was an ice cream in the village on the walk home from church. Later, we went up to the graveyard to visit Francie's grave and to say a little prayer to him. I still have a photograph of Daniel and myself at the grave that day. It was a very hard day for me.

Daniel was prepared for confirmation by his teacher Mrs Logue. She was obviously a very good teacher because he had high expectations of what was going to happen on the day. He thought that he would physically feel something. On the day Daniel was dressed to the nines in a smart suit that Margaret had bought for him with the earnings she got for singing. The suit was too big for him, but Daniel didn't mind. All he could think about on the morning of the big day was how confirmation would change him. He told me afterwards that he watched the other boys and girls going up to the Bishop who administered the confirmation and he was thinking, 'He's got it! She's got it!' He was very apprehensive as he went up himself, but after his high expectations it turned out to be a big let-down for Daniel. He was so disappointed that there was no electricity or anything like that going through him.

Daniel was very popular as a young child, and he was always in and out of our neighbours' houses. He spent a lot of time next door at Josie McGarvey's. Josie's daughter, Annie, doted on Daniel, and he was very fond of her too. She was an adult and treated him like her own son. Annie had a cow, a donkey called Johnny and hens. Whenever Annie was sick, Daniel would put Johnny in the shed in the evening, take in the eggs and turf for the fire, and get her groceries.

Annie was a lovely person and a very popular member of our community. Her big hobby was photography, and she took many of our family snaps, including Daniel's First Communion. Annie had photographs dating back to 1937, the year she first got her camera. We all have fond memories of our dear Annie, who passed away peacefully in 2005.

Daniel loved animals, and he had his own pets around our house, including a pigeon called Jacko, a lovely little, white rabbit, cats and Rover the dog. There was harmony among all the animals. I'd look over at the fireside at night and see the dog, cats, pigeon and rabbit all huddled together as they slept. It was a lovely, warm sight.

When Rover died there was terrible sadness in the house. We all loved Rover. By a strange coincidence, our James arrived home from Dublin an hour and a half after Rover's passing with a wee, white Scottish terrier. He hadn't known that Rover had died. Out of everyone in our home, I think James was the most upset. He might seem like a devil-may-care type, but our James is a big softie really. We put a blanket around poor Rover, and James and Daniel were sent off to dig a grave for him. When they were halfway down the road, James started to cry. He returned home, and it was left to Daniel to dig the grave! We of course then called the new arrival Rover, and he quickly became the centre of attention and a great distraction after the loss of his namesake.

Every now and then I'd give Rover a haircut because he was always going through the fields getting mucky and wet in the ditches. He would sometimes stink like a skunk. Rover didn't like having his hair cut so he used to get very agitated, which made the job very difficult. Eventually I got

tablets from the chemist to make him sleep while I
trimmed his hair. One time he woke up in the middle
of the job, and I had to abandon the grooming,
leaving him with long and short bits.

I then sent one of the children to the chemist for
something a bit stronger to knock Rover out the
next time I was shearing him. When the day
arrived, I gave Rover his tablets and they worked a
treat. I finished the haircut and he was still asleep,
so I put him into a basket in the scullery. The next
morning when I got up, I went to check on Rover and
found him still sleeping away.

Later again I went to look in on him, and he was
still sound asleep. I went over and shook him, and to
my horror I realized that he wasn't in the land of the
living. The tablets had obviously been too strong for
him. I'd given him an overdose. I didn't know how I
was going to tell James. I didn't tell him that I'd
given the dog some tablets. It was years later that
he learned about that dreadful deed. Daniel was
devastated that day and wouldn't speak to any of us.
I felt terrible, but sure it was an accident. In time,
Daniel got over his heartbreak, but there were no
more dogs in our house after that.

There was one cat, however, that neither Daniel
nor the rest of the family had a fondness for. In fact,
I'd go so far as to say that we hated the living sight

of him. He was a big, red, wicked tomcat who had strayed into our home and refused to go away. I did everything to get him out of our house, but he was defiant. Even when a car ran over him, he still survived despite losing half a leg. Talk about a cat with nine lives!

One day I dropped in on a visit to my neighbour Mary Hugo, and I was surprised to find her in floods of tears. 'What ails you?' I asked.

'Och, me poor cats. Me poor cats,' she wailed.

'And what's the matter with your cats?' I asked, trying to calm her down.

'I'll tell you what's the matter. They're all after dying on me. Dying I tell you,' she wailed.

'And what happened to them?' I enquired.

'I'll tell you what happened. There was whiskey poured into the cats' milk and they all died after drinking it,' she sobbed.

My eyes lit up. I couldn't wait to get home and order a bottle of whiskey for the red tomcat. But do you think it killed him? No, he thrived on it! It was some time later before he eventually took the hint and went off to find another family to annoy. He just disappeared, and we never laid eyes on him again.

As I reflect on his antics during his young days, I can see why Daniel went on to become an entertainer.

He always enjoyed being the centre of attention. Many were the times he would put on fancy dress, and then he'd be away through the houses of our neighbours having a bit of fun with them. I recall how one time he went out wearing a wig and sunglasses. He looked for all the world like a young lady, as his outfit also consisted of a dress and shoes with stiletto heels. Daniel called on one old lady in the neighbourhood with a bunch of necklaces and told her that they were for sale.

'And where are you from?' the neighbour asked him, not recognizing Daniel.

'I'm from Japan,' Daniel replied, putting on a foreign accent.

'Have you any children?' the women enquired.

'Six,' said Daniel without hesitating.

'Oh, God save us, give it here to me and I'll buy the lot from you,' the poor woman replied. She went off and got her purse to give him some money.

Daniel then confessed to being in the dress and the wig. Our neighbour, far from being annoyed over Daniel fooling her, thought it was a great joke.

Although he never had to do hard labour, Daniel wasn't totally idle as a child. He did make his contribution to the family by going out to do part-time work in the Cope, which was the local store in Kincasslagh. Everything the community needed could be found in that store, from home-grown produce and tins of food to animal feed and wellington boots! From about the age of nine that store became a part of Daniel's life. I think it really helped him to grow as a person because it brought out his personality and got him used to dealing with people before he went out into the world himself.

Daniel started from the bottom, sweeping the floor and weighing the corn, layers' mash, chick mash and corn cake for the cows. As he gained some experience, he was promoted to a helper on the Cope's delivery van, which went around the high- ways and byways selling goods to people in remote areas. Daniel would come home and tell how people had invited him into their homes to share their food. Betty Doogan was one of the women who'd always have something tasty on the table.

'Och, I got lovely fish fingers in Betty's today,' he'd tell me.

Biddy the Butcher was another woman whom Daniel would mention after his day out on the Cope van. She would often give Daniel and the driver their dinner.

'Och, Mammy, you should taste Biddy's Arctic roll. It's absolutely delicious,' he'd say. It was a sponge cake with ice cream in the centre.

Another day Daniel came home and told me that he had met Protestants.

'And were they nice people?' I asked.

'Oh, Mother, they were lovely. They were just the same as you and me.'

I don't know what impression Daniel had of our Protestant neighbours, but he was very impressed with this particular family called the Boyds when he met them out on the Cope van. I suppose in those times there was no real contact between Protestants and Catholics in the area. Both sides of the religious divide kept to themselves. So that was a good experience for Daniel, to realize that, black or white, Catholic or Protestant, we are all the same.

The Cope employed Daniel part-time throughout his school days, and he really blossomed there. It wasn't hard labour, of course, which suited my Daniel.

Today, he would tell you that one of the chores he hated as a child was working in the bog, when the family set off to cut turf for the fire. He didn't like the labour involved, and there were always midges that would sting. The only part of that day he enjoyed was the lift on the tractor and the lemonade and sandwiches.

At school Daniel was a bright child. I always got good reports about him from his teachers. When he went on to secondary school, I had high hopes of him doing well and going on to get a proper job in life. He often talked about becoming an accountant, which I was delighted about. But I never put any pressure on him to go in a particular direction. I did know, however, that whatever the job would be, it certainly wasn't going to be manual. He couldn't turn his hand to anything manual.

Daniel came home one day and told me that his teacher in woodwork class, a man by the name of Cundy, wasn't too impressed with his handiwork.

'What did you do wrong?' I asked.

'I made a dove-tail joint,' Daniel said.

'And what was wrong with that?'

'I thought it was good myself, but Cundy didn't think so.'

'What did he say?' I wondered.

'Well, when I asked him what I should do with it, he told me to throw it in the fire,' Daniel sighed.

Poor Daniel. He would often say in jest, 'I might as well not have been born with hands – they're only there to finish off my arms.'

While I always allowed my children to find their own feet in the world and didn't push them in any partic-ular direction career-wise, there was great concern among some of our neighbours about what was going to become of Daniel. One local woman, in particular, who fretted over his future was Nora Dan, who lived up beside the graveyard about 2 miles from our home. Nora was a very good-natured person and very hospitable. There were always callers to her home – and not always of the human species. Her hens would wander into the house as well and jump up on the table when you were having your tea. 'Shush! Who invited you,' she'd say, sweeping them out the door with her hands. Nora used to come up to the shop every Friday to get her pension, and then she'd come to me for her dinner and her tea.

One day the conversation came round to Daniel's future. Nora was desperately trying to come up with a job that might suit him.

'Maybe he'll go to the bank?' Kathleen suggested.

Nora shook her head, instantly dismissing that notion. 'Sure you wouldn't be able to afford laces for your shoes till you were a bank manager. And there are so few bank managers. You'd be working as a clerk, and sure what they're paid isn't worth talking about.' Nora paced up and down her kitchen, shushing the hens out the door again. 'Do you think would he make a good Garda?' she thought out loud.

Before Kathleen could offer an opinion, Nora answered herself. 'No, no. You need good sight to be a policeman, and Daniel has anything but good sight in one of his eyes. If there was a robbery in the village, he might have to read the getaway car from a distance, and sure with his bad eyesight he'd be a dead loss. No, the Garda's not for him.'

Nora gave up. 'What's going to become of him?' she sighed as she flopped back onto a wooden chair by the fire. As far as she was concerned, Daniel was going to have his work cut out to make it in life. Little did any of us know what lay ahead for him.

chapter ten

My Lovely Island Home

I WAS AT home in Kincasslagh, looking out over the sea, as I pondered on Owey's fate. Daniel was due in from school, and as I cooked his dinner the tears were rolling down my cheeks.

There had been a dark cloud hanging over me all morning. It was the day that the remaining islanders were packing their belongings and leaving Owey for good. For the first time ever, there would be no light and no footsteps on Owey. The island that had reared so many families would no longer echo with the sound of children playing. There would be no music and dancing echoing from the hooleys in the hall.

Owey had been made redundant as people left for the comfort of mainland life. You couldn't blame them, but I was heartbroken to think that the island was going to be deserted and the remaining cottages left to fall to ruin.

Of course, by this time my own family had gone from the island. My father, God rest him, passed away on 28 January 1963. He was 86 years of age, which seemed old to me at the time. Now that I'm writing this book at the age of 86 going on 87, it doesn't feel that old at all. It's funny how the older you get the younger people become. Now I would say that he was only 86 when he passed away.

My father had been a fit and healthy man right into his final years. Even at the age of 80 he was up on the roof of our little island home, doing insulation work on it.

There was one time when he was suffering from a cold on the chest. He had the doctor check it out. The doctor told him that treacle was very good for a chest complaint. So my father got the treacle and rubbed it on his chest.

'You know, this is a shocking bad treatment. Sure the clothes are sticking to my chest,' he told me.

'How would they be sticking to your chest?'

'Sure that treacle is terrible sticky stuff.'

'And what did you do with it?'

'I rubbed it on my chest,' he said, pulling at the clothing on the upper part of his body.

I laughed. 'Sure that's not where it goes at all. You're supposed to eat it,' I explained.

'Oh,' he nodded. 'Sure the doctor never told me that.'

Then he laughed at the thought of his own foolishness.

To me, my father was one of the greatest men that ever lived, and I was heartbroken when he died. A neighbour, Pa Logue, who ran a local shop and bar, came up to the house to tell me that he was sick. There were no phones at that time. The Cope store would deliver messages over to the island. It was through the Cope that word came back to Pa that my father had taken a turn. By the time I reached Owey, I could see that he was close to death.

Up to that moment, my father had always been afraid of dying. There was many a time growing up on the island when I heard my father say that he would be afraid to die. But when the time came, he was at peace with it. The local priest came over and anointed him, and my father said he wasn't one bit afraid of going to meet his maker. After seeing the priest, he was happy. On his death bed, he announced, 'I'm going to die now and I haven't one thing to be afraid of. I've done nothing to nobody, and I'm going to die now real happy.'

My father's greatest fear during his lifetime was that my mother would die before him. He just couldn't face being in this world without her. They were such a united couple. They were very happy together. I'm sure they had their bad days like everyone else, but people in those times made their marriages work and were much happier for it. They didn't move on to somebody else when the going got tough, like they do in modern times. I can honestly say, though, that I never heard a cross word passing between my mother and father.

It was the end of an era when my father took his last breath. As fate would have it, I wasn't there when he passed away. I had gone back to my home in Kincasslagh to get the family sorted out. I had just crossed over to the mainland in the currach when he died, and it was the following morning before I got back.

Then a storm blew up, and on the day of the funeral it caused a lot of problems on the crossing from the island to the mainland. The currach carrying the coffin had to go way off the normal course to find a calm spot to land. In those times there were no cars and no hearse, so the coffin had to be carried from the seashore to the church, which was a long trek from where the currach had landed. There were six men at a time taking turns to carry the coffin on their shoulders to the church and, after the funeral Mass, to the graveyard in Cruit for burial. It was a long, sad journey for all of us, particularly for our mother. At the age of 85, she had lost her life-long partner. It would be eight years before they'd be reunited in the next world.

*

After my father was buried, I took my mother over to Kincasslagh to live with us. She would return to Owey for a short visit in the summer for many years afterwards, but she spent the rest of the time with me. She never got over my father's death. She pined for him right to the end of her own life. I recall reminding my mother five years after his passing that it was Daddy's anniversary that day. 'Indeed I know, and five long years it's been,' she replied. They had been like two peas in a pod. Every Sunday evening during the summer they always went for a walk together to see how the crops were growing. When they came back home it was time to say the rosary, so we all went down on our knees and joined in.

Despite her great age, my mother continued to be an industrious person. You'd always find her sitting in a corner of our house, knitting socks. There was a man called Whoriskey who used to place orders with women in the locality who were interested in making a bit of money from knitting; my mother was one of his team of knitters. He then exported the socks. He'd call to the house to collect the ones she'd finished and give her more wool for the next batch. It gave my mother a sense of financial independence and a daily purpose in life. Knitting kept her occupied right up to the end of her days.

In her final years, my mother suffered from

arthritis in her knees, but otherwise she enjoyed good health. One day the two of us were sitting each side of the fire, and both of us were knitting. Suddenly my mother's knitting fell to the floor, and when I looked over at her I knew by her face that she'd had some kind of a turn. I caught her two hands and stuttered in a panic, 'What's wrong with you?'

She didn't answer, but I knew she was bad. I quickly put her in a comfortable seat and ran to ask my neighbour, Biddy Tague, to come over quickly and stay with her. Then I raced to the village to get the doctor and the priest.

The doctor was the first to arrive, followed shortly afterwards by the priest. After the priest anointed my mother, a strange thing happened. She picked up the sock she was knitting for Whoriskey and finished the toe on it. It was her last knitting job. She'd suffered a stroke.

My mother was 93 years old when she died on 15 July 1971. I minded her in her final days and prayed that I wouldn't get sick with flu because then she'd have to go to hospital. I wanted to be with my mother till she passed away, and I'm so glad that I got my wish. She had been one of the oldest surviving islanders, so a lot of history went with her when she died.

Mother really loved Owey, and even at the age of

90 she went back to the island and spent a week living in the old homestead. She put on a pair of men's wellies and stepped into the currach which was to take her across from the mainland. I contacted the local paper to write a wee bit about her visit to the island on that occasion because she was 90 years old and it was quite an achievement. She got cross with us for going to the paper, but I knew she was secretly delighted.

Although my father and mother were now gone, I still couldn't bear to think of Owey being completely deserted. On its final day as a home to families, I finished making Daniel's dinner and left it simmering in the pan for him. I wiped tears from my face with my apron as I thought about all the good times I'd had on Owey. Time does play tricks with your mind, because the bad times never seem so bad with distance.

As the memories took me back to my young days, I thought how it was odd that nobody had ever written the story of Owey Island. Priests had come from the island, and nuns and teachers. But not one of them had ever written anything about it. And as I pondered on this, the words of a poem started going around in my mind. I got a pen and in a flash I wrote the following:

As I sit here sadly thinking
How the years go swiftly past
My thoughts go back to my childhood days
When I was but a lass
And we a happy family
Gathered around our turf fire bright
And the fairy tales our parents told
On the cold, dark winter nights
My brothers they are married now
With families of their own
My sister lives in the USA
In her grand Long Island home
She pays a visit now and then
To greet us one and all
Still our thoughts roll back to those happy days
In our home in Donegal
But our island home lies empty now
The clock hangs on the wall
The fireside chair it still sits there
There's a padlock on the door
The raging seas and the wintry winds
And the seagulls weary cry
No fire burns bright in our hearth tonight
As it did in days gone by
So fare thee well my island home
Where we spent many happy days
And fare thee well to my friends so dear

Across the ocean wave
May God protect and bless you all
Wherever you may roam
For Owey was like heaven to us
In our happy island homes.

To this day that poem is etched in my memory. I don't need to write it down to remember it. It's there, and I can recite it at the drop of a hat. I called it, 'My Lovely Island Home'.

When Daniel came through the door that day, I said, 'Come here, Daniel. Wait till I recite this to you.'

Afterwards, he said, 'Mammy, you didn't write that.'

'I did, Daniel,' I said.

'Well,' he said, 'you should get that published in a paper.'

So I sent it to our local paper, the *Donegal Democrat*, where it was very well received. There wasn't a *Democrat* left on the news-stand on the day it came out in the locality. When the local teacher, Master O'Donnell, went down to the shop to get his *Democrat*, the paper had been sold out. People were buying it to send the poem to their families abroad.

*

Now Daniel has turned that poem into a song, and it's on his album, *Until the Next Time*, which was released in October 2006. I was very proud that he should see fit to record it and to keep Owey's memory alive. The CD has been bought by Daniel's fans all around the world, so our lovely wee island is now world-famous.

Sadly, our island home is derelict; nature has been slowly chipping away at it, and the house is overgrown with weeds. It was always a lovely house to me. I used to have the interior walls as white as snow with brown borders on the bottom.

The last time I saw my dear old homestead was in a video my daughter Margaret made for one of her songs. I didn't recognize it because it was in a bad state. If I'd known Margaret was going to put it in a video I would have had it painted. The video was lovely, but the old home that held so many happy memories for me was a sorry, empty, decaying shell. I was very sad to see it in such a state; it brought tears to my eyes.

chapter eleven

A Star is Born

D URING HIS SCHOOL days I became aware that Daniel had a great love of people. I didn't know then just how far his popularity with folk would spread. But I recall one incident that made me realize I had a very special boy.

Daniel would travel by public bus to and from secondary school in Dungloe. One day, after shopping in the town, I returned on the same bus with him. As we waited to board, the driver said: 'Let all the schoolchildren stand back now while the adults get on and get seated.'

Daniel said, 'Mammy, you go on and if you see everybody seated keep a seat beside you for me.'

So I went away up to the middle of the bus and found myself a seat, with a spare one beside me for Daniel. I heard some people behind me saying, 'Danny's not getting on.' I thought they were talking about one of their own. I glanced round and it was a man and a woman, an elderly couple who were neatly dressed, well groomed and both had beaming, friendly faces.

Then my Daniel appeared at the door of the bus, and I heard the lady saying in an excited tone, 'Oh, Danny's on.' And Daniel came down the aisle of the bus wheeling a trolley. I thought to myself, where in the name of God did he get the trolley? He came down to where I was sitting, and then he left the trolley standing alongside the couple behind me.

Daniel sat down beside me and the lady said to him, 'You're not sitting beside your girlfriend today.'

And I said, without looking back, 'Oh, but he is sitting beside his girlfriend.'

The lady asked, 'Do you know Danny?'

'Well, a good right I should have to know him,' I said.

She asked, 'Do you live near him?'

I told her I did.

'Don't tell me,' she said in an excited state, 'you're not his mother by any chance?'

'I am, that's who I am,' I replied.

'Well, do you know this, you must be the proudest mother in Ireland today,' she said. And she told me their story and the difference that Daniel had made to their lives.

'We came down from County Down in the North because we were afraid of the Troubles. We bought a little house down here. Every so often we go up with this trolley to the supermarket in Dungloe for our groceries. Before Daniel came to that school up there, some of the youngsters used to kick the trolley in front of them in a stampede. Sometimes it would tumble over onto the road and the groceries would all be tossed out. Since the day Danny first saw us, he took the trolley off us and made us go on and get a seat on the bus. Then he would take the trolley on and leave it beside our seat. And when he would be getting out at Kincasslagh, he would take the trolley to the door of the bus to leave it handy for us when we were getting off at our stop. He is such a lovely, considerate young boy, we absolutely love him. Now that's my story about Danny.'

All the pensioners had a similar tale to tell about Daniel. 'Our hearts will be broken the day he leaves that school. Daniel is always helping us on the bus with our bags. And if there's one of us who needs support getting in and out of the bus, it's Daniel who steps up to lend a hand. That boy has so much good in him. He would make a good priest; oh, he would be a lovely priest,' they would say.

Daniel, of course, would sit there red-faced with embarrassment whenever he heard anyone paying him compliments like that.

Daniel had a lovely singing voice as a child, and, just as I did with Margaret, I always encouraged him to use it. There were singers on both sides of his family but particularly on Francie's side. Francie's mother and father had lovely voices. Every one of Francie's sisters and brothers could sing. So Daniel didn't lick it off the ground, as they say. It was in the genes.

Whenever there were concerts in our local parish hall, I would always take Daniel down to sing. The priest would invite him up on to the stage, and he would perform for the crowd. I remember the first song he ever sang was called 'Little Cabin Home on the Hill'.

One time there was a local talent competition in Castlefinn and I brought Daniel along to enter it. That was his first time ever performing in a talent contest, and he came second. On another occasion while we were on a visit to County Mayo, Daniel entered a local talent event and won it. He was only eight years old at the time, but he was beginning to cause quite a stir. The crowd in Mayo thought he was something special. Everybody was saying to him, 'Oh, you are going places.'

It's not that I was pushing Daniel towards the stage. I had no dreams of him becoming a profes-sional singer. I just saw it as part of his growing up, something that would give him confidence. It takes a lot of bottle to go out and sing in front of a crowd.

Even though he was my youngest child and I was left on my own to bring him up after Francie died, I didn't smother Daniel. I kept a close watch on him during his very young years, but as he got older I let him find his feet in the world. I allowed him to go away on holidays to relatives and friends. He used to go to Arranmore Island and stay with a cousin of ours, Agnes Sharkey, who originally came from Owey. She had married an Arranmore man and settled on that island. I recall how Daniel once spent six weeks there. He would go up to Sligo and stay with Ita Carney, a friend of Margaret. I never worried about him because I knew he would be safe with the people he was visiting. I'd send him off on the bus, and somebody would meet him at the other end of the journey. Some of the money he earned working in the Cope during his schooldays covered the expense of a holiday every year in Scotland, where he stayed with relatives in Glasgow, Edinburgh, Perth and Callendar.

Daniel loved his visits to Edinburgh, and I remember him coming home after one holiday and telling me a story about the cuckoo clock in the city's Princes Street. The cuckoo would come out of the clock on the hour, as I recall, and Daniel was fascinated with that. It was something of an attraction in Edinburgh, and a crowd would gather to watch it.

'Mammy, do you know what, that cuckoo isn't real at all. I always thought it was until last week when I heard some of the crowd saying it was a great invention! And I loved that cuckoo,' he said, shaking his head in disbelief.

One time Daniel came home from Edinburgh with a lovely pair of shoes that had gold tips. He was a real dandy in them and couldn't wait for Mass to come round the following Sunday when he would give them their first public outing.

Coming out of Mass a local lad said to Daniel, 'They're a fine pair of shoes you're wearing.'

Daniel's face lit up with pride.

'And they're a quare good bargain too at £4.99,' the lad added.

Daniel stopped in his tracks and asked, 'How do you know what I paid for them?'

The local teenager pointed to the sole of one of the shoes. Daniel checked it, and there was the sale sticker still on it. The whole chapel full of people had seen it when he knelt down at the altar to receive Communion. 'Isn't that shockin' embarrassing,' he said later.

As Margaret became more and more successful as a singer, she shared her good fortune with the family. In 1972, she even sent Daniel and myself off across the Atlantic by plane to visit my sister Maggie and many other relatives in America. Margaret had gone over there the previous year to do a tour and she had met a whole army of our relations. A big party was arranged for Margaret in New Jersey, and everyone who was related to us came along. She realized that night that I would love to have been at the party surrounded by all those family members, most of whom I'd never met. So she decided before she came home that she would send me out.

She'd also left the party that night with a bag full of envelopes. People would go up to her and say, 'I'm a cousin of your mam's' and slip her an envelope. The next day when Margaret opened them she found that they were filled with cash, and the whole lot came to about $500. It seems everyone among the family connections in America was aware that I'd been going through hard times. They all wanted to give a little to help Julia back in Ireland. And I really appreciated their kindness, particularly as $500 was a fortune to me. I'm sure every family throughout Ireland has a similar story to tell. The American cousins, even though they might not have been to Ireland themselves, never forgot us all back home on the old sod. And they'll never be forgotten for their generosity.

The following year I found myself on a plane for

the very first time in my life. A trip to the States was
a major undertaking way back then. You'd spend six
months preparing for it and another six months
getting over it. Nowadays I hear of Irish people
going to New York for a weekend to do their
Christmas shopping. How times have changed. But
that trip to America over 30 years ago was worth it
for many reasons, not least being the look of excitement on Daniel's face. If Margaret had sent him on
a space shuttle to the moon he wouldn't have been
more excited. Not many people of Daniel's age – and
not many of my age group either – got the chance to
travel abroad in those days. A trip to America was
really out of the ordinary, unless it was to emigrate.
It was the talk of the whole community around
Kincasslagh that we were off to the United States of
America on a holiday.

  I wasn't looking forward to the long journey on
the plane, but I was excited because it had been
such a long time since I'd seen my sister, who was
living in Bayonne, New Jersey. I said the rosary as
we took off from Dublin, praying for a safe journey
across the Atlantic Ocean. I had been frightened
going onto the plane, and I wouldn't sit at the
window because I was afraid to look out. But once
the plane took off and the journey was under way, I
settled down. It was a long, long trip, about seven

hours, but I dozed off for a time so that helped it to go by quicker than I imagined. Eventually the captain announced that we were on our descent and before long we were safely on the ground at John F. Kennedy Airport. I crossed myself in thanksgiving for a safe passage as the plane came to a halt, and I couldn't wait to get off and meet up with Maggie.

It was an emotional reunion and a very happy time for us. Maggie wanted to know all the news from home and what had changed since she'd left. There was a litany of births, deaths and marriages to fill her in on, not to mention how the area had been transformed since she'd emigrated, with new homes springing up here and there. Maggie lapped up all the stories, and, as we reminisced, all the memories came flooding back; it was lovely to share them with everybody.

The red carpet was rolled out for us, and shortly after we arrived there was a big party organized so that we could meet all our relatives and their friends and neighbours. I remember how there was a big table in the middle of the floor and it was creaking under the weight of bottles of drink. Most people at the party were having a drink, but I had never touched alcohol in my life. People would come up to me and say, 'Will you have a drink?' And I'd tell them that I didn't drink. 'Would you not take a drink of 7UP?' someone asked me. I didn't know what 7UP was at the time, and, thinking it was alcohol, I refused. Daniel became the centre of attention, and all eyes were on 'the cute young Irish boy', as I heard someone remark. Daniel even sang for them. He performed 'Little Cabin Home on the Hill' and 'The Philadelphia Lawyer', and there were loud cheers and lots of back-slapping when he finished. He was beaming with pride.

Daniel and myself spent a total of six weeks in America on that trip, and we visited many relatives, including Bill and Margaret O'Donnell. Daniel was very happy there and he enjoyed the company of their children, John and Bridget Mary, who were around his age. He even accompanied them to school one day on a big yellow bus, a visit that caused quite a stir among the American schoolchildren. When he returned home later in the afternoon, Daniel told me that all the young Americans had been going on and on about how they loved his accent. 'Gee, would you speak for us?' they would ask. He loved all the attention.

I was like a child myself on that trip as I discovered things I'd never seen before. Like cranberry sauce. One day when we sat down to a turkey dinner I saw the cranberry sauce on the table and I presumed it was jam. I thought it was very odd when

I saw everyone digging in and putting this 'jam' on their turkey. When I got nobody looking I dipped my finger in the jar and tasted it. Well, it was lovely, so ever since then I've been a fan of cranberry sauce.

My daughter Margaret had a boyfriend who was working in New York at the time, and she came out for a visit while we were there. It was a surprise for Daniel and myself when she walked through the door. I look back now on that period with a lovely warm feeling. That was a great holiday for us, and I'm so glad that Daniel still has those wonderful memories of our time together in America.

On our return to Ireland, Margaret was waiting to collect us at Shannon Airport. At that time there were no restrictions on the amount of luggage you could take with you on the plane, which was just as well because I think I brought half of America home with me. I took everything that was given to me while I was on holiday. There were people throwing out trash, or what they called trash, but it was real good stuff to me, so I offered to take it off their hands and home it all came with me. I remember Daniel going up to Margaret in the airport at Shannon and saying, 'God, Margaret, we've an awful lot of stuff!'

There was a carnival dance that night in Killala, County Mayo – it was in a marquee – and Margaret was performing with her band. So we packed everything into her car at the airport and off we headed for Killala. The car boot was stuffed, there were cases and bags tied onto the roof with ropes, and you couldn't see Daniel in the back with all of the bits and pieces that were packed around him. I don't know what the fans must have thought of Margaret when they saw her car pulling into Killala that night with what looked like all her worldly possessions.

Margaret remembers that show for another reason. During her performance she invited Daniel up on stage to sing 'Little Cabin Home on the Hill', and she says it was the moment she realized that he had something special about him. Margaret had heard Daniel singing before, of course, but she had never seen an audience react to him like they did on that particular night.

My first inkling that Daniel was thinking of following in Margaret's footsteps came in 1980, when he went to college in Galway city, where I thought he was studying to go on to be a teacher or an accountant. I was delighted that he was pursuing something that would give him a good living and that had security, because I knew from Margaret that the music business was far from easy. I would have loved to have seen Daniel go on to become a teacher because I think he would have been an excellent one. He was always so good at communicating with people, and he's a great listener. I think he would have inspired people to do their best, and he would have given them the confidence to strive for their highest goals.

I have to admit to being very sad and concerned about his welfare seeing him leaving for the Regional College in Galway. Even though he was 18 years old and had already been out in the world a bit, including spending that summer of 1980 washing dishes in the kitchen of a Dublin hotel, I was afraid that something might happen to him. In Dublin he'd stayed with his brother James, but at the time I was always concerned about him whenever he went to any city. I used to be frightened that he'd get killed crossing the road. When he moved to Galway, it was very hard on me because I missed him terribly, and I still miss him to this day when he's away. But you have to let your children go, whether you like it or not.

The only thing that eased my worry was the fact that I knew he was staying with very nice people, Sean and Pat Nugent. They were a lovely couple, and Daniel would tell me how they treated him like one of their family. Even so, he didn't settle into college life in Galway.

At first, he used to come home every third weekend. Then it became every weekend. And that was a marathon journey. The public bus used to take him up to Donegal town; then he'd have to hitch the remaining 40 miles to Kincasslagh. After a time, I began to realize that it wasn't just his love of home that was bringing him back. He didn't like it in Galway at all, even though the Nugents were so nice to him. I think he didn't fit in well with college life. By the time Christmas came, Daniel had already made up his mind that he was going to leave and join Margaret's band.

Coming up to Christmas, Daniel had already spoken to Margaret about becoming a singer. They had discussed it when he went along to one of her shows in Galway. Although she didn't discourage him, Margaret's advice to Daniel was to give it serious consideration.

Whenever he performs himself in Galway these days, Daniel always loves to tell the audience how Pat Nugent, the lady of the house where he stayed, had also given him advice when he told her that he was leaving to become a singer. 'Wouldn't you be better off learning something first?' she'd responded. It always gets a laugh, including from Pat, who never misses his shows.

To be honest, I was very concerned about Daniel

leaving college to join a band, even though it was Margaret's. But at the same time, I didn't interfere, although I did ask Daniel to be sure that he knew what he was doing, and would it not be better if he did something else. James also tried to discourage Daniel from going into Margaret's business.

'Look where he is today and to think that I tried to stop him,' James says now.

Young people have to find their own way in life, make their mistakes and make their fortune, good or bad. Daniel could not be persuaded to give up his dream, so on 28 January 1981, he stepped out onto the stage behind Margaret at a venue called the Rag in Thurles, County Tipperary. It was his first performance as a professional entertainer. He had joined Margaret's band as a rhythm guitarist, except he couldn't play guitar, so it wasn't plugged in. But that was the start of his apprenticeship, pretending to play a guitar in his sister's band. 'I had to start somewhere,' Daniel always remarks whenever anybody mentions it to him.

When I reflect on it now, I realize that Margaret had a huge influence on Daniel's early adult life. He developed his stagecraft from watching how Margaret performed and how she communicated with the audience.

Daniel got a real buzz from performing with Margaret. He saw how the music and the singing created so much excitement and joy for people, and he grew to love the applause. He never did learn how to play that guitar.

The following April, Daniel played his last show with Margaret at the Longford Arms Hotel in Longford town and started out on his own journey in music, not realizing just how far it would take him.

As his career began to take off, he moved to Dublin, and I went with him. Margaret was living in Galway because her band was based there, but she also owned a house in Ballinteer on the south side of Dublin city.

'Why don't you go into my house instead of getting a flat?' she suggested to Daniel as he made plans to move to the city. 'Sure you'll have it for nothing, and in any case I'm worried that someone will break in and squat in it.'

He was delighted with Margaret's offer, and a week after that we both moved in. I didn't want Daniel to be away on his own with nobody to wash his clothes or cook for him. We both settled into the house in Dublin, and it was a good time for us. It was a home from home for Daniel, and he always looked forward to my cooking, especially my apple tarts and pancakes.

During those early days Daniel didn't have much money. He couldn't afford a car, and he didn't even have a bicycle. But he never asked anything of me because he knew I didn't have any money either. It's not that he would want to be buying things anyway. Material possessions weren't important to him, and still aren't to this day.

We arrived back from the city centre one day and there was a note under the door, with a message asking Daniel to ring a particular number.

'God, Mammy, I don't know whose number that is,' he said.

We had no phone in the house, so Daniel headed off on foot to the nearest phone box to make the call. He returned soon afterwards to say that the phone was out of order. He then said he would take the bus into the local village of Dundrum and make the call from there. It transpired that it was a Wexford woman who was desperately trying to contact Daniel. The woman and her friend were big fans and had been to all of his shows since he'd started. The Wexford woman told Daniel that her friend was dying and that she kept crying out, 'Daniel, Daniel, Daniel.' The woman pleaded with him to come and see the poor lady. Of course, he went as soon as he could organize a lift.

I don't know what it is about Daniel that draws

people to him in that way. What I do know is that he has brought so much happiness and comfort to many people since he became a singer. Throughout his career, he has gone out of his way to call on the sick or people in need for whatever reason. And he has made such a difference to the lives of those people. Daniel has told me time and again that he feels privileged to be in a position to have that effect on others. It has been a really rewarding experience for him. And, as his mother, I am so delighted that my Daniel has been able to bring so much sunshine into the lives of others.

I travelled a lot with Daniel during our time in Dublin. He'd be going off with Ronnie Kennedy from the band and he'd say, 'Sure why don't you come with us? You might as well, instead of sittin' at home on your own.' He didn't have to ask twice.

But I wasn't totally dependent on Daniel for company during my time in Dublin because my son James, his wife, Eileen, and their family were there – as was my dearest cousin, Willie McDevitt. We had a very strong bond, Willie and myself. We were more like a brother and sister. Willie used to always say to me, 'You're the one cousin out of all the cousins that I like the best.' He was a kind and gentle man. Every summer for many years Willie and Rose came up to our house in Kincasslagh for their holiday. We didn't have much space, but we made up beds on the floor, and they always enjoyed their time with me.

Willie was a chef by trade, and as our James grew up he too showed a great interest in cooking. And it wouldn't be normal dishes like bacon and cabbage or beef stew. James would be experimenting with meat and vegetables and making up dishes of his own. My mother was living with us at the time, and she was the one who would sample whatever he baked. I'd often see her scooping the last of the juices off her plate with a finger, she was a big fan of James's cooking.

When Willie came on holidays to us during the summer, he was very impressed by James. 'James would make a great chef, Julia,' he'd say to me. Then he said to James one time, 'If you want to go on to be a chef, come to me and I'll get you started.'

The summer that James left school at 14, I went on a short visit to one of Francie's sisters in Scotland, taking only Daniel with me as he was too young to leave behind. When James got me over in Scotland, he packed a bag and went away to Dublin to Willie. The first I knew of it was when I came home.

'James is gone,' Kathleen said, and I knew by her tone that it wasn't to the local shop.

'Gone where?' I asked, almost afraid to hear the answer.

'He's gone down to Dublin to Willie to be a chef,' she told me.

I was shocked but at the same time relieved because I knew he would come to no harm once he was under Willie's wing. I was heartbroken to lose him, and I cried for weeks. James was so much fun around the house, and I missed his trick-acting.

'Don't you worry about him, Julia. Rose and myself will look out for James. He's a good lad and he'll go far in life,' Willie reassured me.

James said later that he knew, if he'd asked me, that I wouldn't have let him go to Dublin at 14. And he was right. But now that he was there, I put him in the care of Willie and gave him my blessing.

And so began James's outing in the world on his own. Willie started him off washing saucepans and peeling potatoes, and gradually taught him the trade of being a chef. James worked his way up the ladder until he was as good as Willie himself.

As soon as Daniel and I moved into Margaret's house in Ballinteer, Willie came to visit us every day, even if it was only for a few minutes. He'd be checking to make sure that everything was all right with us. Family meant everything to Willie.

I have so many happy and funny memories of Willie during that period in Dublin. I recall how one time it was snowing outside and the path to our house was covered in mucky slush. So when I saw Willie's car coming up the road, I raced into the kitchen and got a bundle of newspapers to spread in the hallway where we had a pink carpet. Willie would always come in through the hallway and go over and sit in our armchair. I spread the newspapers the whole way from the door to the armchair so that the pink carpet wouldn't get destroyed. When Willie came in, he began to lift the newspapers, and he lifted every one of them and laid them down in a neat bundle beside the armchair. He passed no remark about the papers, and I didn't say why they were on the floor.

Some time later, I heard how he'd said to Rose when he arrived home, 'Do ye know, Julia is getting very untidy.'

'Why do you say that?' Rose asked him.

'There were newspapers scattered all over her floor. I had to tidy them up,' he replied.

I laughed when I heard that.

Sometimes Daniel would drop me off at Willie's home when he went away, and I'd spend the evening with him and Rose. We got on well together, Rose and I. She was like a sister to me. I always liked her.

As soon as I walked through their front door, Willie would go off and get me a pair of slippers. 'Take off your shoes, now, and make yourself comfortable while you're here,' he'd say.

One night while I was in Willie's house I told him that I had to go into St Vincent's Hospital the next day for a check-up.

'It's a pity you're not going into Vincent's in a couple of days because I have to go in myself and the two of us could have gone together,' Willie replied.

On the day I arrived at St Vincent's I saw Willie's daughter, Rosita, and Rose sitting there. What are they doing here? I thought to myself. I went over to them, and I could see by Rose's face that she was very upset. Willie had been rushed to hospital. He was dying. Whenever I think about that day, I always think how it was such a strange coincidence that I had to go into the hospital at that very moment.

When I went in to see Willie I realized that he was in a very bad way. He had an oxygen mask on his face, and when I went over to the bed he removed it, put his arm around me and gave me a kiss. I didn't stay long so as not to tire him, and as I was going out the door he shouted, 'See ya!'

That night I stayed with Rose at their home. We

were sleeping in separate rooms and at 3 a.m. a knock came to the door. The two of us rushed down the stairs. Willie was dead.

chapter twelve

Tea Day

MY EARLY WORKING life in the fields and fishing ports of Scotland was so different from the lifestyle that Daniel would go on to enjoy. That's not to say, of course, that Daniel didn't work hard for everything he achieved, or that he didn't have tough times in his early days. It might seem like a glamorous life, but the reality is so different.

Sometimes there were more people on the stage in Daniel's band than there were on the dance floor, and he was barely making ends meet. At the time, of course, I didn't know how much of a struggle he was experiencing. As far as Daniel was concerned, I didn't need to know; there was no point in two of us having to worry about his future in the entertainment business. It was only much later that I heard all of the stories.

While travelling across England, Scotland and Wales, he and the band often had to sleep in one room at motorway lodgings because that's all they could afford between the lot of them. The band members drove their own unreliable, battered old van, with Daniel taking his turn behind the wheel too. But he never got disheartened. Daniel persevered because he loved what he was doing, and he believed that he could succeed. I think there's a lesson there for everyone. Find something you love to do in life and you'll always do a good job. Stick with it even during the times when it seems hopeless.

I was always worried about Daniel, and I said a rosary every night that he would meet good people in the music business who would look after him and guide him. Eventually, my prayers were answered. The two Irishmen who changed his life were Mick Clerkin, who gave him a big recording deal, and Sean Reilly, who became his manager. I always remember Mick and Sean in my prayers today because they have been so good for Daniel. Sean has been like a father to him. I don't know what Daniel would do without Sean guiding him. A man with a kindly schoolmaster's appearance, Sean is quietly spoken and a real gentleman. There are so many terrible stories told about singers being abused and diddled out of their earnings by unscrupulous managers, but Sean Reilly has honesty and integrity. Whatever Daniel was entitled to he got and not a penny less. Not only that, Sean had great vision and a belief in Daniel's talent, and that would take them further in show business than most people ever imagined – they would even go on to do very well in America. Daniel put his total trust in Sean, and he has never been let down by his long-time friend.

With Mick and Sean looking after him, it wasn't long before Daniel was filling the dance venues all over Ireland as well as England, Scotland and Wales. The word was spreading that this boy was something special, and before long there were queues waiting outside the dance halls several hours before he was due to perform.

In the years that followed, Daniel enjoyed more and more success, and I was delighted for him because I could see that he treated singing as a vocation. Daniel devoted all the waking hours in his life to his role as an entertainer. When he wasn't travelling and performing, he was writing letters and cards to fans or going off to meet people who were sick, just to give them a little boost. It was no bother to him. Daniel loved every minute of it.

Whenever I'd go to his show, I'd see the joy that Daniel created among the people there, and that was a good feeling for me. Daniel would always take a moment during the evening to tell the crowd that I was in the audience; then I'd have to stand up and give a little wave.

'Look at her waving; they wouldn't do it any better

in Buckingham Palace,' he'd say, and the crowd would all laugh.

And then a strange thing happened; the people who followed Daniel started to recognize me. They would stop me to chat about Daniel and to have a photograph taken with me. Not just people from Donegal or Ireland but people from all over the UK as well. I woke up one day and realized that I was a bit of a celebrity myself. Now that's something I'd never imagined as a child running wild around Owey.

I became aware that people were pointing me out when I was going into Daniel's shows. 'There's Daniel's mother,' I'd hear them say. I was very happy to be recognized as Daniel's mother. It made me feel good because I was proud of what he was achieving in his life. And the whole county of Donegal was proud of him too.

One evening in 1989 we were on our way back to Donegal from Dublin. We were travelling along Gweebarra, a stretch of road between Maas and Leiter, in County Donegal. Although there were no houses along the road, we came upon a lot of cars that were parked.

'What's wrong here?' Daniel wondered.

'There must be a wake somewhere,' I said.

'How could there be a wake when there are no houses?' he remarked.

Daniel was driving swiftly along and the next thing he spots a Garda car waving him down. 'Oh,' he said, 'I've been caught driving too fast.' When Daniel stopped, he discovered that the Garda and all of the other people were there for him. He had been voted 'Donegal Person of the Year'. There were hundreds of cars out to meet him. Even though it was pouring with rain, all of those people came out for Daniel. I was so excited sitting beside him in the car that evening.

I still have that citation he received on behalf of the people of Donegal. It reads:

Daniel O'Donnell is a perfect example to the youth of our county and country. Success has not gone to his head. He has never forgotten his roots. He has not forgotten his mother and his family. He has not forgotten his beloved Kincasslagh and Donegal. And above all, he has not forgotten the people who have put him where he is today – his loyal fans.

He is never too busy to stay behind after shows to talk to them and sign autographs. Many are the stories that could be told of his visits to homes and hospitals to visit sick fans, even when that meant interrupting busy schedules.

One story which aptly displays his concern for his fans is the one which tells of an occasion when it came to his notice that some fans who were travellers (Irish gypsies) were being refused admittance to his show. He refused to go on stage until they were admitted.

Daniel never loses an opportunity to lend his name and his services, if possible, to worthwhile charities.

A non-drinker and non-smoker, his clean-cut image in his dress and in his living standards does not meet with approval from some of the gurus in the media, who seem to wish he were otherwise. But they meet with the approval of us here in Cumann Tir Chonaill (County Donegal).

The people who chose Daniel as their 'Donegal Person of the Year' recognized that he's a great ambassador for his native county. During his concerts he always paints a wonderful picture of the place he comes from, and he's forever inviting people to come and visit Donegal and Kincasslagh.

One day I woke up to find 600 fans outside my house – and they'd all been promised a cup of tea by Daniel!

For many years, during the local 'Mary from Dungloe' festival, Daniel would hold what he called an 'Open Day' at our house, where he'd meet anyone who wanted to see him. Daniel's fans came to the festival from all over Ireland and Britain, and as far away as Australia, New Zealand and America.

One evening before the Open Day I noticed a car parked over at the bend near our house, and I could see a couple in it. Some time later I saw that it was still parked at the spot. 'I wonder what they're doing sitting there?' I remarked to my daughter Kathleen.

'I don't know, but they are there a long time. I'll go over to them to see if there's anything wrong,' she said.

The couple told Kathleen that they were going to stay there for the night, so that they'd get first place in the queue to meet Daniel the following day.

Kathleen was astonished. 'Do you want me to bring some blankets out to you?' she asked.

'No,' they replied. 'We have our blankets and everything else we need for the night.'

When I got up the next morning, the couple were sitting on the wall by the road. I made tea and pancakes and took it out to them. They were so delighted, and we chatted for ages and ages. Daniel has really lovely fans, and they're so devoted to him.

On one of those days I met another couple who were just married, and they'd decided to make Daniel's Open Day at our house part of their honeymoon experience. Wasn't that lovely!

Daniel should have called his Open Days 'Tea Day at My House' because everyone who came to see him got a cup of tea. Kathleen and all her crew kept the tea flowing, and one by one the fans passed through, greeting Daniel, having their photos taken and getting their cuppa. It was a lovely day for everyone.

All our neighbours were very understanding too, because I have no doubt that the traffic jams were a nuisance for them at times, even though the local Garda were on duty trying to keep it all running smoothly. No one ever complained, though, I have to say.

Eventually Daniel had to bring an end to that event. In the early stages, hundreds came to meet him. By the end, there were 6,000! And television crews from Ireland, the UK and even America! That was an incredible amount of people to cope with. And it looked like it would get even bigger. Daniel realized then that the Open Day had become a far more popular attraction for the fans than he ever anticipated. People were waiting too long in the queue. And then Daniel could only give them a few seconds. He felt that the fans were going away disappointed, so for everyone's sake the curtain had to come down on it. But the memories of that time are great.

I will never forget the sight that would greet me when I'd look out of the windows on the morning of that Open Day and see thousands of people. It was unbelievable. To this day fans sometimes stop at the house when they're visiting the area and I often meet them. They sometimes ask me to step in for a photograph with them, and they say, 'You are the next best thing to meeting Daniel.'

I also get lots of letters, sent to me personally by Daniel's fans. And they come from all over the world. I try to answer most of them, even though I'm sure nobody expects me to write back. These days I have all the time in the world, so what a lovely way to pass it by keeping in touch with people who have such a love for Daniel.

chapter thirteen

Doolittle and Diana

WHEN I WAS growing up, my mother used to say to us that we should never feel there was anyone out there in the world who was better than us. In other words, that we should never feel inferior to anyone else, regardless of their status in life. She'd sip from her cup of tea in the evening after we'd eaten and tell us, 'There's nobody in the world who's better than another person. Everyone was born as clean as the other, so there's no difference between any of us.'

Through Daniel I have met all kinds of people – the rich, the famous and ordinary folk like myself. And I have always remembered my mother's words. As a result, I've been neither nervous nor excited about any other person.

When Daniel got his own TV show in Ireland at the end of the 1980s, many international stars were among his guests. But it wasn't just Daniel who got the opportunity to meet them – I was always brought backstage and introduced to them too.

As fans of Daniel know, he loves the American country legend Loretta Lynn. So imagine his excitement when he was told that Loretta had agreed to come to Ireland to appear on his show.

Never mind what my mother used to say about nobody being better than you, Daniel was a nervous wreck when Loretta arrived in Dublin to perform with him. Although he doesn't normally get flustered, even when the world is collapsing all around him, he was acting like a turkey at Christmas before meeting Loretta.

Loretta was a lovely woman, though. She probably spotted that Daniel was nervous, but she was so funny and kind and without any airs or graces that he soon settled down. The pair of them then sang 'How Great Thou Art'. It was really lovely. Later, I was taken to the dressing room at the TV show and Daniel brought me in to meet Loretta. She was a very striking-looking woman in the flesh. She had piercing blue eyes and Cherokee cheekbones. She was really warm and friendly. I had made a batch of pancakes especially for her, and when I gave them to her she was so thankful. 'Oh, you are such a sweetheart,' she said, giving me a hug.

Loretta had had a very hard time herself during her early days, as I discovered when I'd gone to see *The Coalminer's Daughter*, which was a very good and honest film about her life. I discovered how she came from a really poor background, just like myself, in a place called Butchers Hollow, Kentucky. She had been married at 13 and a mother at 14, and by the age of 18 she'd given birth to four of her six children. By the time she reached 30, Loretta was a grandmother, as well as one of the biggest stars of country music. I really admired how she had turned her life around from such a tough start, and how she had battled through everything that life threw at her to achieve great success while remaining a very grounded person.

Loretta's husband, Doolittle, came to Ireland with her for Daniel's show. And I'll tell you, I wasn't too impressed with him after watching the film. He'd been a bit of a jack-the-lad who'd been carousing with other women behind her back.

Someone pointed out Doolittle to me in a back-stage area, and suddenly I was reminded of the film and the story of their life started running through my head like a show reel. I remembered that Doolittle didn't even have a ring to give the young Loretta on their wedding day. As I looked him up and down that day and caught his eye, I couldn't think of any redeeming feature about the man – he wasn't even handsome.

I eventually sidled up to Doolittle and gave him a

piece of my mind. 'You were a right boyo!' I said.
'Hadn't you the cheek to marry that nice girl and no
ring with you!' Well, he couldn't get away from me
fast enough. Daniel was mortified when he heard
what I'd said to Doolittle. He and Loretta had been
engrossed in conversation at the time.

Many years later, that incident caused Daniel great
concern when he learned that he was going to
receive an award from Prince Charles.

On the morning of New Year's Eve 2001, we woke
up to newspaper and radio reports that Daniel had
been awarded an honorary MBE by the Queen of
England. Apparently a large number of his fans had
written to Queen Elizabeth telling her about
Daniel's charity work, particularly his involvement
in a Romanian charity that had been helping to
improve the quality of life for the poor unfortunates
of an orphanage in a town called Siret. One of our
neighbours, Eileen Oglesby, had been working in the
orphanage, and she had told Daniel about the in-
humane conditions those young people were forced
to endure in that terrible place. They were sleeping
30 to a room, both boys and girls, in a run-down
building. It was a house of horrors.

During his time in power, the dictator Nicolae
Ceauçescu had ordered that every family in Romania

should have five children. But parents couldn't afford to support families of five, so they dumped the children in those orphanages. Daniel decided to record a single called 'Give a Little Love' and donate all the profits to this charity. Before releasing the single, however, he went out to Romania to make a video for the song. He had no thoughts of becoming involved in the charity at that time, but he told me later that once he arrived there and saw at first hand the shocking conditions that those unfortunate human beings were living in, he knew that he couldn't walk away from them. The stories he told about what he witnessed on that first visit to the orphanage sent shivers down my spine. Daniel says he'll never forget the awful stench that greeted him as he entered the building, and the pitiful sight of young people who had been locked away and forgotten by the world. Many of them, he said, had suffered terrible disabilities from being confined; their heads were shaved, and they spent their time rocking back and forth. They had nothing to stimulate them and no one to show them love. He said that many of them went to him and hugged him. They didn't know Daniel, but they would hug anybody who showed them any kind of warmth and attention.

'Give a Little Love' was released in April 1998 and was a great success in the charts, both in

Ireland and in Britain. Daniel went on to use the stage and his fame to draw people's attention to the suffering of those people, and through his shows he encouraged fans to support the work of the charity by making donations. A collection was organized at each of his concerts.

In the years since then, wonderful things have been happening in Siret. The charity is now involved in farming and has built homes to give the people of the orphanage the opportunity to have a normal life.

It's not that Daniel did any of this for some sort of recognition. It's just something that came into his life by chance. But it was taken into account by the Queen when she awarded him an MBE. Daniel was delighted when he heard the news because he felt that getting an MBE would mean so much to his English fans. That their Queen was recognizing Daniel was the greatest honour they could have given him. And the fact that it was coming from his fans as well as the Queen made it an award for Daniel himself to treasure.

Some time later, Daniel received an invitation to the British Ambassador's residence in Dublin, where the MBE was to be presented to him by Prince Charles. Daniel was allowed to take some guests, and that's how I found myself in the company of His Royal Highness, the Prince of Wales.

Before the special occasion, however, Daniel warned me to be on my best behaviour. He didn't want a repeat of the Doolittle incident. You see, Daniel knew that I worshipped Princess Diana. For some reason I became a fan, not something I normally do. But, like so many other people, I took a real shine to her. I even kept a scrapbook of stories about her. I saw something special in her, saintly even. She used her status and fame to support the underprivileged, the downtrodden and all kinds of worthy causes. She was good to people of every race and religion. I saw her visiting children who were suffering from AIDS and all kinds of illnesses, and she would lift them up in her arms. I could see that she was a genuinely caring person. And I thought she was the most beautiful girl in the world. Nobody else came close.

Naturally, I was upset for Diana when her marriage fell apart. Her wedding had seemed like a fairy tale. This was a real live Prince and Princess who looked so much in love. But all wasn't as it seemed, and the fairy tale didn't last. That saddened me. And then, of course, there was Diana's tragic death in Paris. I cried for a day when I heard the shocking news. My daughter Margaret phoned me from London that morning to tell me. I was devastated and my heart went out to Diana's two boys. Some time later I wrote to the boys, and I received a reply thanking me for my letter.

I was aware that Daniel was worried about me meeting Prince Charles. He was delighted that I was allowed to accompany him to the big occasion and happy that I was still alive to witness it. But knowing my devotion to Diana and remembering how I had chastised Doolittle, he was on tenterhooks in case I'd have a go at Charles about his relationship with Camilla. He warned me not to saying anything that might offend the Prince. I heard later that he'd said to Margaret, 'She's liable to say anything, you know.'

The first thing I noticed about Prince Charles was his beaming smile. Next I noticed that he's not as tall as he looks on the television. I'd always thought he was very tall, but he's much smaller than I imagined. He was very dapper in his smart suit, very charming and easy to like. I could see that, despite being a member of the royal family, he had a common touch. He moved slowly through the room joking with people as they greeted him. He seemed to be a very easy person to be around. As he was getting nearer and nearer to me, I'm sure the family members with me were becoming more and more anxious. Finally,

Prince Charles was standing before me and I heard Daniel saying, 'This is my mother.'

'How lovely to meet you,' the Prince said.

I smiled and replied, 'How is your granny?' At that time there had been reports that the Queen Mother wasn't very well.

'She's marvellous, marvellous ... doing very well,' the Prince replied.

'I'm delighted to hear that,' I said.

Prince Charles thanked me. And then he kissed my hand before moving on to meet the other MBE recipients in the room.

I was charmed. And I'm sure that my son, Daniel O'Donnell MBE, was relieved.

On the journey by car to Donegal that night, my mind wandered back to my young days on Owey. Suddenly I was a child running barefoot along the stony paths to check on the cows. It was a world away from royalty and the grandeur of the embassy building where I'd just spent the evening with Prince Charles!

chapter fourteen

The Wedding

ALTHOUGH MATERIAL POSSESSIONS have never interested Daniel, his success has allowed him to enjoy some really nice things in life. They include his own lovely island home on Tenerife in the Canaries, where I've been a regular visitor in latter years. It's so good to go there and get some heat into my old bones.

Daniel loves Tenerife as a place to go and relax in the sun after his tours. And of course it's really special to him today as it was there that he met Majella.

For many years, one of my prayers was for Daniel to find someone nice who would love him and look after him as I'd always done. There were a couple of times when it looked like those prayers were going to be answered. But sadly it didn't come to pass. I always said I would die contented when I saw him happily married.

I knew that Daniel's life as a travelling singer made it difficult for him to meet someone special, as he was never in one place for very long. And I knew that it's not every woman who could live with an entertainer's job. Singers like Daniel who do lots of touring are away from home for long periods. They give a lot of their lives to the people who follow them. It's not a big sacrifice for them, of course, because they get a lot back in return. But it's not easy for a wife and family to deal with that kind of a life and those times of separation.

As the years passed and Daniel's 40th birthday was coming up, I really thought he would remain married to the stage for the rest of his life. He had moved back from Dublin to our home in Kincasslagh, where I was living with my daughter Kathleen, her husband, John, and their children. Daniel had built his own living area at the rear of the house over-looking the sea. He seemed to be very happy there, so I thought that he was going to remain a bachelor. Little did I know that he'd cast his eye on someone in Tenerife in 1999.

Daniel had met Majella, whose father and mother, Tom and Marion Roche, ran a bar on the island. It was a while before I was told about this big romance because he was concerned about how I would react. Majella had been married previously and was the mother of two teenage children. Daniel knew that didn't sit well with my religion.

One day my daughter Margaret told me that Daniel

had a girlfriend and filled me in on the background. Margaret had been to Tenerife, had met Majella and was very impressed by her. At the time of that conversation, Margaret and I were preparing to go out to visit Daniel in Tenerife for a short holiday.

'When you meet Majella will you try to put behind you the fact that she's divorced?' Margaret said to me as we packed our suitcases. 'Daniel's happiness means a lot, and they will be good for each other,' she stressed.

I didn't know what to think on the plane journey. I was in a state of confusion because, while I wanted Daniel to be happy, I was afraid that he would get hurt.

Majella came to meet us at the airport. The first things I noticed about her were her big smile and friendly eyes. She was tanned and looked very well in her white slacks, red blouse and flat, comfortable shoes. She said hello, gave me a hug and helped me with my suitcase. Majella was a warm human being; in fact she was a nice country woman from Thurles in County Tipperary.

Later, when she was around Daniel, I could see that they were happy together. He looked very relaxed in her company, and they shared the same sense of humour. There was a lot of laughter in the room when they were there. At the time, Daniel didn't say anything to me about his relationship. I suppose men, particularly sons, are not good at that kind of thing.

We had a really nice time during that visit, and on the way home I remarked to Margaret, 'Majella is a lovely girl. It's a pity she's married.'

Margaret laughed. 'Mother, she's not married. She's divorced.'

Daniel chose 12 December 2001, the night of his big 40th-birthday charity banquet at the Hilton Hotel in Birmingham, to introduce Majella in public as his girlfriend. I sat at the top table with them, and I could see that she was nervous about the announcement. She was sipping a glass of white wine to steady herself.

There were 1,200 people in the banquet hall that night when Daniel went up to the stage after the meal and told them that he had someone special to introduce to them. I'm sure many of them thought it was going to be me, because no one knew at that time that he had a girlfriend. You could have heard a pin drop when Daniel told his fans that he had found someone that he wanted to spend the rest of his life with. He told them how happy he was, and he expressed the wish that they would accept her as part of his life. Then he introduced Majella.

I have to admit that I shed a little tear as I sat there listening to Daniel talk about the special woman in his life. Up to that moment, I had been that special woman; it's not easy for a mother to let go.

On Christmas Day, Daniel and Majella had us over for dinner at the lovely home he'd bought at Cruit overlooking the sea, with Owey in the distance. I was there with my daughter Kathleen, and her husband, John, and a few friends. Daniel suggested to Majella that she should go up to their room and phone her mother in Tenerife before we all settled down for the meal. Within a few seconds, Daniel followed Majella, and I assumed that he wanted to wish Tom and Marion a happy Christmas.

After a short time, Majella came back to the dining room and her face was flushed. She looked like she'd been crying. Daniel was just behind her and he was beaming.

'Folks,' he said, 'we have just got engaged.'

Daniel had surprised Majella with an engagement ring, taking the phone from her as she spoke with her mother. He told Marion what he was about to do, and Majella burst into tears.

I burst into tears too when Daniel broke the news to us. Everyone got very emotional, but we were happy for both of them.

Some time later Daniel and Majella announced

to the family that they had set the date for their wedding: 4 November 2002. I have to admit that, while I was happy that he was happy, I still had a lot of misgivings about Daniel marrying Majella because she had been married before. So I was praying that he had made the right decision.

The wedding day was one of the saddest and hardest times of my life because I was losing Daniel. I cried all day. I was happy for him that he had found someone to share his life with, despite my misgivings, but I was feeling so sorry for myself. To add to my woes, I woke up on the morning of the wedding suffering from some kind of a bug. I was feeling poorly. I was also in a lot of pain because I had burnt my foot on a hot-water bottle in bed the previous night. A big blister had now come up on it, and I wasn't able to put on the new shoes that I'd bought for the wedding. It wasn't a great start to the big day for me.

The house was a hive of activity that morning. Daniel had observed tradition by spending the night apart from his bride-to-be and had slept at our house.

'How did you sleep, Daniel?' I asked him when he popped his head round the door at breakfast time, thinking he was going to say that he'd had a bad night because of the excitement and nerves over the wedding ceremony.

'Well, I'll tell you not a word of a lie, Mother. I slept soundly,' he said.

I could see that he was in good spirits, and there were no signs of any nerves. Not that he got much time to think about it with all the fuss. Family members were in and out of the bathroom, the girls were busy doing their hair and make-up, and then Daniel's party, the best man and groomsmen, arrived – his childhood friend P.J. Sweeney, his nephew John Francis and our James. They were all looking very smart in their wedding suits.

The wedding was set for 1 p.m. in our little parish church in Kincasslagh. Daniel was anxious to have everyone there on time because Majella had told him she wouldn't keep him waiting for long. She'd be there at five minutes past the hour.

Entering our lovely little church I was in a very emotional state. There were so many memories for me in that church. It was there that Francie and myself had married. The tap was on and the tears were flowing.

I was in my seat and the church had filled up with all the guests when Daniel came through the door and over to the front pew. He had a smile from ear to ear coming in, but when he saw all of us – his family and friends – gathered under one roof for his wedding, he suddenly burst into tears himself. 'God, I don't know why I'm crying,' he said as he greeted everyone.

Finally, Daniel sat in the groom's spot at the top of the church as we waited for the arrival of Majella. The minutes ticked away and Daniel shuffled anxiously in his seat. Occasionally, he glanced at his best man's watch. After 20 minutes, he was looking a bit worried. After all, Majella had warned him to be on time. By this stage, we were all getting a bit restless.

Finally, word came through on someone's mobile phone that there had been a hitch. Majella was trapped behind the electric gates at their home. Daniel wasn't the least bit ruffled by this setback. I think he was relieved that there hadn't been an accident and it was something that could be sorted out. To pass the time, he sauntered up and down the aisles greeting all of his guests.

Another 20 minutes went by before Majella finally arrived, and, as the wedding music struck up, the floodgates opened again. Hearing Daniel and Majella take their vows was a moment I had prayed for, but I'd never considered that it would be such a wrench for me.

*

Daniel's wedding caused a big stir that day, even though he hadn't turned it into a show business affair by inviting lots of stars. Hundreds of his devoted fans came along to the little churchyard and waited patiently in the rain to see the happy couple. The wedding Mass was very long, but they still kept a vigil out in the cold and the rain. There were photographers peeping out from behind head-stones in the graveyard, and later I was told that Sky News had been broadcasting live from outside our church. You'd think it was a royal wedding it got so much attention.

As Daniel and Majella and the rest of the guests travelled in a convoy that evening from Kincasslagh to the town of Letterkenny, where the wedding reception was to be held in a local hotel, bonfires were blazing along the route and locals braved the heavy rain in honour of the happy couple. It was really lovely to see how much people still cared for Daniel in his home county. I was very proud; it lifted my spirits because I was feeling very poorly on the journey due to the bug I'd picked up. All I wanted to do at that moment was to get into a nice, comfortable bed.

At the hotel I could see that Daniel and Majella had put a lot of thought into their big day. The flowers in the banquet room were just beautiful, and people stood to admire the wedding cake. Our neighbour

Eileen Oglesby, who had introduced Daniel to the Romanian charity, had made the cake. It was designed like a fountain and was a real work of art. It was a shame to slice it up.

Later, during the reception, Daniel made a wonderful speech, and if I had any doubts about his feelings towards me, well, he put them to rest when he spoke that evening. I cried over his beautiful words when he said, 'I was six when my father died and from then on my mother has been everything to me. She never let me feel that I needed anything I couldn't get. She gave me security, she gave me love, and she gave me encouragement to sing. When I started singing I was always going to tell the world how wonderful she was, and she will always be that same person, that wonderful woman who was such an influence in our lives.'

Today, I am the happiest mother and mother-in-law alive. Any concerns I had about Majella at the beginning have been put to rest. She has been good for Daniel. I think she is great. Majella has given Daniel a wonderful life away from the stage. They are a happy couple who enjoy their time together. It is so lovely to see him settled and content.

Majella is very good to me too, and we are the best of friends. I even gave her the secret recipe for my famous pancakes. That's something I never gave another person, so I suppose that says a lot about our relationship and what I think of her. Daniel joked in an interview one time, 'When I saw my mother teaching Majella how to make pancakes, I knew she was ready to let go.'

chapter fifteen

That's Life

THEY SAY YOU have to experience the bad times to appreciate the good ones. As I sit here today looking out over the rugged coastline of Donegal and reflecting on times past, a golden ray of sunlight shining through the window of my room, I realize how true that is. I thought when Francie died that I wouldn't be able to carry on in this world without that wonderful man in my life. I thought that was the end of my life and my happiness. It seems a lifetime ago that Francie was taken from me. It's a long time to have to live on memories. And nothing will ever take that sadness out of my life. It will remain with me until the day I die. I loved my husband more than I can ever express on paper. Sometimes when I sit at home alone I keep thinking what he would be like if he had lived. Would he look much older? My tears fall at the very thought of him being here with me, and of the happy times I would have if we were still together. The only consolation I have is that I know he's in a happy home with God. But never a day passes that I don't think of him and wish that God could have spared him.

Life can beat you up if you let it. But a sense of duty can turn you into a fighter. I was left behind with the enormous responsibility of having to rear and watch over a family. In that situation I didn't have any other choice but to put my heartache and my worries aside and get on with the job. Humans are truly wonderful beings really. We are a lot stronger than we give ourselves credit for. It's only when life tests us that we realize just how good we are at meeting those challenges. And, for me, having my religion and my faith in God was my greatest source of strength. It got me through many a dark hour and day. I also prayed to Francie to give me the strength to carry on, and I know he was with me as the years rolled along.

Although God closed an enormous door when he took Francie away, he opened up so many other doors to me. I've seen my children grow up, leave the nest and go out in the world to make lives of their own. Here I want to tell them how much I love them and how blessed I feel to have reared such fine people. They have come through all of life's struggles, and I am proud of every single one of them. I love them dearly, and I'm so lucky to have them in my life.

The first of my family to get married was John Bosco to Bridget, and the night before his big day he wrote me a note telling me what time to call him that morning. Believe it or not, I still have that little note from 21 October 1975. I treasure those last few lines John Bosco wrote to me as a single man.

James was the next to marry. He wed Eileen on 23 October 1976, at the age of 18. Even though he's been in Dublin from the age of 14, James has never forgotten his dear old mother. He keeps in touch with me and he gives me good laughs. He's a very comical fellow. He'd often come up to Donegal to visit me without warning. I'd go into my bedroom and he'd be lying in the bed under the covers, and then he'd jump up and give me a fright. It was always a nice surprise for me. That's James's sense of humour.

One time somebody asked James, 'What's it like to have a famous brother?'

James replied, 'I don't know; you'd better ask Daniel.' He has done very well for himself in Dublin, where he is one of the owners of a famous pub called Cassidy's on Camden Street. I'm always very happy to see him, even if it's only for a few hours.

My daughter Kathleen married John Doogan on 28 April 1979. Kathleen and John have always been very good to me. We've shared the same home, and

I've had happy times in that family. So, Kathleen and John, it's something I really do appreciate.

I have seen Margaret and Daniel become famous and celebrated around the world as popular singers. Fans often said to me, 'You must be the proudest mother in the world.' I'm reluctant to say that I'm a proud woman, even though I'm delighted with everything they have achieved, but I know that anything they got, they got from God. Their voices, those are a gift from God. Margaret and Daniel went on to give me a wonderful gift by bringing me into their worlds. That gave me experiences in life that I never dared to imagine.

John Bosco, Kathleen and James have also given me another wonderful gift – grandchildren. And I adore them all. There's John's sons, Frankie and Joey; James's sons, Paul and Christopher, and his daughter, Margaret; and Kathleen's children, John Francis, Patricia, Fiona and Daniel. There is nothing more precious in the world than children and grandchildren.

And now I'm even a great-grandmother.

In October 2005, I was sitting in a well-positioned balcony seat looking out over the audience who were enjoying one of Daniel's greatest shows at the Point Theatre in Dublin. I had one of the best views of the stage, and it was one of those special nights I didn't want to end. I was watching Daniel's dream come to life. He had created a big rock 'n' roll show. It was no ordinary concert – this was a big musical, and Daniel was the star as well as the person who had dreamed it up and brought it to life right there before my eyes. He had never done anything like this before, but you wouldn't have known it that night. He had everything on the stage, including a Cadillac and an American diner. At times I thought I was watching a movie. It was just spectacular, and it was being filmed for PBS television in America.

When the interval came round and the lights went up, I thought I couldn't handle any more excitement. I could see by the expressions on the faces of Kathleen and Margaret that they were just as thrilled. They were chatting excitedly among themselves, and I thought they were discussing the show. Then Margaret whispered in my ear and what she told me brought an even bigger smile to my face. I got the best news ever; I had just become a great-grandmother. My grandson Frankie and his lovely wife, Lisa, had just become parents for the first time. Lisa had given birth to a lovely little daughter they called Sarah.

When Frankie was born I became a grandmother for the first time. Now he has made me a great-grandmother by bringing little Sarah into this world.

It seemed like it was only yesterday that Frankie was just a child himself. He used to come over to me every weekend and how I loved those visits.

I recall how one time I took Frankie over to a nearby lake to show him a family of swans that were swimming gracefully by the shore. I brought a little bag of bread with me for Frankie to feed them. Then I sat on a hill and took out my knitting while he went down to the lake to throw the bread out to those beautiful birds. It was quite shallow by the shore, so I didn't have any major concerns about him being down there on his own. Somebody had left a wee, tin boat and nets by the side of the lake, and he began to play with them. I continued knitting and felt proud looking at Frankie having all that fun.

Just as I was enjoying the moment I saw Frankie slip and fall into the water. He got such a shock that he jumped up and ran up to me in floods of tears.

'Look what you did to me, Granny! I'm all wet and I'll be killed by Mammy,' Frankie wailed.

'Don't you worry, Frankie, I'll take you home and we'll dry your clothes,' I said, trying to calm him down.

So off home we went, Frankie shuffling along in his wet gear, sobbing his little heart out. When we reached home, I put on a big fire and took off Frankie's clothes and hung them to dry. As soon as they were ready, I helped him to dress again and prepared him for home.

'Don't tell your mammy and she'll not know a thing. Then she won't give out to you at all,' I said before he left.

That night when his mother, Bridget, was taking off his clothes, she asked, 'Frankie, did anything happen to you today?'

'No,' he replied.

'Well, your vest is turned a different way to the way I put it on this morning,' Bridget pointed out.

Frankie then confessed all, so I was caught out!

And now he has a child of his own, and he loves that wee Sarah. We all do.

Great-grandmother: I never thought I would see that day. It makes me sound awfully old, but I suppose it's about time I realized that I am what they call an old person. It's a description that doesn't sit easy with me. In my own mind I'm still a teenager racing around Owey Island. The old legs don't carry me as far or as fast these days, but the mind is still young. Does everyone of my vintage feel like that? I wonder. I believe they probably do. It's what keeps us going and up with the times.

*

Now that I'm in my twilight years my thoughts often wander back over my life, and it lifts my heart to think that I haven't got an enemy in the world, at least none that I know of. There is no person out there that I have a grudge against, and I don't think there's anyone who bears ill will towards me. And that is a good feeling.

It's lovely to bump into people unexpectedly and to have them remind you of some good event in the past. I recall how one day I was travelling back to Donegal on the bus from Dublin and we stopped off in Cavan for a break at a local café. When I stepped inside the door I met Charlie Boyle, who used to be a teacher on Owey. That was at that time when my mother used to make a pot of cocoa and leave it in the hot ashes by the fire for us to have when we were going to bed. Every night during the week Charlie would drop in to have a cup of cocoa and share crab toes with us. When I went into the café in Cavan that day, Charlie was there with his lovely wife. We reminisced over old times – and he treated me to tea and scones as a little thank-you for my mother's hospitality. It was a lovely moment for me.

I know too that the times have changed for the better in a lot of respects. Work isn't such a hardship any more for the young or even the old – well, in this part of the world anyway. And that's a good thing.

Even though I'm not ashamed of where I came from and have no regrets, I wouldn't like to see my grand-children having to do the kind of work I did when I was young. Young people in general today have a nice life, but I wonder: do they appreciate it? And when I see so many going off the rails, I wonder: are they really better off today in some ways? In my young days you wouldn't dare speak back to your mother or father, or any of your elders, because you knew that you'd feel a sally rod across your legs. And that would be the last time you'd do it. Thank God I never spoke back to my parents. I respected them as parents should be respected – and I was spared the sally rod!

Now that my parents are gone, I pray for them every night. And I pray for my brothers, James and Edward, who died in recent years. I pray a lot these days, and I don't forget anyone who is ill. I think you should always remember the people who are suffering or in pain. They all need prayers. People of today don't pray enough. When we were young, you were made to go on your knees as soon as you got out of your bed to say your prayers, and the same at night before you went to sleep. You said your prayers and a rosary every night with all of the family present. Where did all those religious customs go?

When someone died on the island of Owey, people sat up all night at the wake, and candles burned day and night. It concerns me that it's not like that today. Nowadays the lights and the candles go out at midnight, and no one keeps a vigil out of respect for the body in the coffin. When I die, I hope that the lights don't go out. I want people to be with me for my last two nights at home. So many traditions, religious and otherwise, are no longer observed today.

For all the downs that I've had with my husband not being around, and the loneliness I've experienced as a widow, there have been more ups. I know in my heart and soul that God has been more than good to me and that I've been more fortunate than most. I've seen the world and met all kinds of wonderful people, and to this day I am in contact with people from all corners of the globe, fans of Daniel. There's hardly a day goes by that the postman doesn't drop cards or letters through my door from some of Daniel's fans.

On my last birthday I got 126 cards from Daniel's fans all round the world. And many, many parcels of gifts arrived at my door. I couldn't reply to them all, so I'll do my thank-yous here and now. I love the fact that at my age I still have a connection with so many people. It keeps me going. I am blessed that

I'm not hidden away and forgotten. I am still getting great enjoyment out of life through Daniel and the rest of my lovely family.

I thank God that things turned out so well for them. We struggled along through the hard times and we kept in close contact. My family are all able to do their own thing now, and I keep an eye on them. I suppose I will always know that I'm an influence in their life, and I hope they listen to me when I try to keep them doing good. But I have no problems with anything any more. All is going according to plan for me and them, and we get on well together. It's a happy family, and what more could I ask for?

So, when my thoughts wander back to yesteryear, I think of the hard times and the sad times and so many happy times.

It's what we call life.

And that was my life.